Up And Running In Real Estate Sales

by P. J. Thompson, G.R.I.

Kricket
Publications

Santa Barbara, California

LIBRARY OF CONGRESS
CATALOGUING-IN-PUBLICATION DATA

Thompson, Pauline J., date

Up And Running In Real Estate Sales.

Includes index.
1. Real estate business--United States.
2. Real estate agents--United States. I. Title.

HD255.T49   1987   333.33   87-16916

ISBN 0-918785-02-2

HD
255
T49
1987

Printed in the United States of America.

First printing: 1987

Table Of Contents

Figures

OTHER KRICKET BOOKS BY P. J. THOMPSON:

Real Estate Farming: Campaign For $uccess

Santa Barbara: How To Discover America's Eden

Introduction

Real estate is a profession which has a very high number of dropouts; most of these are agents who do not survive even the first year. Everyone comes into the business with high hopes for a satisfying, rewarding career and those who do drop out seldom know why it eluded them. It is my opinion that the blame can be evenly divided between the inadequacy of pre-licensing courses, non-availability of proper training or guidance in too many real estate offices and the lack of initiative on the part of failing licensees to educate themselves by other means.

Pre-licensing courses are packed with information about metes and bounds, titles and estates, and other material the student will need to know to pass the licensing examination but do not cover the nuts and bolts of listing and selling real estate to make a living. The profession assumes that, because your broker is responsible for your actions, that person will provide all the on-the-job training and advice you need. Many brokers do offer good leadership and education but there are others who are now so distant from their own beginnings in the business that they have forgotten how much they had to learn. They are surprised to be asked what seem to them very basic questions and their reaction causes some agents to hesitate to seek further help from this source. It is difficult for an agent to become a self-starter without knowing how to proceed.

You have every reason to be confident about your future in real estate if you know what to do and when and how to do it. This book was written for both new licensees and those who are hanging in after a year or two just managing to survive on a combination of the odd commission check and their savings. By reading it and following the advice it contains, you will learn to become a self-starter and how to achieve success. All aspects of finding, acquiring, marketing and selling listings are covered. Guidance is given on how to work effectively with buyers, sellers and those equally important people, your peers. Agents with some experience will find many useful ideas to enable them to improve their performance. The book will answer many of your "how do I ....?" questions and the detailed index which follows the last chapter will direct you quickly to pertinent material when you need it for reference during transactions in the months ahead.

No matter what field of work one is in, a typical social question is, "How long have you been in ....?" Although you may think otherwise, the inquirer is probably not doubting your competence but is simply making conversation. Once you have acquired the necessary knowledge and are competent to take a buyer or seller through a transaction (even if it is the first time), that question should no longer give you a feeling of inadequacy. You will do the job well and gain confidence in your abilities. As one successful transaction follows another, you could become a member of an elite group of true real estate professionals, (the top twenty per cent who do ninety percent of the business.)

While real estate is a serious affair and this is a serious book, there is always room for a little levity. The amusing sketches reproduced in this book appeared in the popular British magazine, "Punch", between 1841 and 1914.

Welcome to the wonderful world of real estate sales. Let's turn now to Chapter One and get up and running on the road to success.

Pauline Thompson
Santa Barbara, California

1

First Days
On The Job

*C*ongratulations! You have a brand-new real estate license and a sparkling future. It's your first day at the office. You've been introduced to a few associates, given a desk and suddenly you're on your own.

The life of a **productive** real estate agent is hectic. There is never enough time. Every minute is precious and not to be wasted. The following activities are some of the ways in which your working days will be spent:

1. Listing and selling property;

2. Working with customers or clients;

3. Working with other agents;

4. Contacting potential customers or clients;

5. Cultivating your farm;

6. Updating your real estate knowledge;

7. Attending meetings;

8. Previewing properties;

9. Holding Open House;

10. Floor time

Plan Your Work, Work Your Plan

To keep up with all these activities and the hundreds of details involved in a real estate transaction, it is essential to be well-organized. Develop the good habit of writing EVERYTHING down that is to be done and check each item off (or cross it out) as you go along. By preparing daily and weekly "To Do" lists, you are planning your work and then working as called for by the plan. Your first "To Do" list can incorporate the following activities:

TO DO LIST #1

1. JOIN THE LOCAL BOARD OF REALTORS AND/OR MULTIPLE LISTING SERVICE

2. OBTAIN A COPY OF THE CURRENT MULTIPLE LISTING CATALOG

3. OBTAIN A SUPPLY OF REAL ESTATE FORMS

4. PREVIEW PROPERTIES CURRENTLY LISTED BY ASSOCIATES IN YOUR OFFICE

5. PURCHASE AN UP-TO-DATE STREET MAP OF YOUR CITY

6. PURCHASE DAYTIMER & OTHER TOOLS OF THE TRADE

7. HAVE PHOTOGRAPH TAKEN

8. ORDER BUSINESS CARDS AND STATIONERY

9. ORDER NAME RIDERS AND SIGNS

Read the following explanatory paragraphs and then get busy!

1. Join the local BOARD OF REALTORS and/or MULTIPLE LISTING SERVICE

It is essential that you participate in MLS. This gives you the privilege of:

> (a) inserting your own listings in the regular catalog (weekly in most markets);

(b) receiving a copy of each issue to use to locate suitable properties for potential buyers;

(c) access to such properties;

(d) attending agents' marketing meetings.

In some States, the multiple listing service (MLS) is operated as a service of the Board of REALTORS and your broker must be a member of the Board to enjoy MLS privileges. In others, such as California, MLS is a separate entity and your broker has the option of membership in both Board and MLS or of choosing either one. You, as a licensed salesperson, will usually be required to follow membership policy set by your broker.

The National Association of REALTORS is located in Chicago, Illinois. Each State has an affiliated Association of which local level Boards of REALTORS in the State are members. Part of the fee for membership in your local Board goes to the State Association and part to the National Association. Your local Board office will have literature for you explaining the valuable services offered by the three entities and you will quickly see the advantages offered and prestige gained via your Board membership.

2. Obtain a copy of the current MULTIPLE LISTING CATALOG

Your broker may have given you a copy of the current catalog (also known as the MLS or multilist book). If not, ask for one at the Board office when you join. Ask, too, if copies of back issues of the "Sold" books are available for purchase; it is useful to have a reference set of these for the past two years for your home office bookshelf.

Study these books to become familiar with current listings and to make yourself aware of prices at which similar properties have sold. Note the layout of the book and data it includes.

Go over every one of the forms used by the MLS service to enter new listings and report on their status. It is handy to make a checklist of all information the service will require from you when you are submitting a new listing for publication. Take it with you for reference when you do a listing presentation so that you can collect all necessary data from the seller during your visit to the home.

3. Obtain a supply of real estate forms

There are printed forms for every type of real estate transaction. Local custom, or State law, determines which ones are used in various locales. The forms include, but are no means limited to: Listings; Offers to Purchase; Counter Offers; Addendums; Contingency Releases; Exchanges; Occupancy Before Close of Escrow; Lease With Option; Competitive (or Comparative) Market Analysis; and Disclosures. Listing forms alone can come in several varieties depending upon the type of property, form of agreement, etc. Ask your broker now for current samples of forms most commonly used; you can familiarize yourself with the others as your career progresses. A supply of current real estate forms may be available at your office for the use of its agents, from the local Board of REALTORS or your State Association. A limited number of office stationery stores and printers stock forms and mail order sources include: California Association of REALTORS, 525 South Virgil Avenue, Los Angeles, CA 90020; and Professional Publishing Corporation, 122 Paul Drive, San Rafael, CA 94903.

Some State regulatory agencies, such as California Department of Real Estate, include samples of forms in common use in the pages of the reference manuals which they publish. In Colorado, where licensees are required to use only those forms officially appproved by the State Real Estate Commission, every form is included, no less than 43 in the 1986 edition.

When I began work in real estate in the 1970's, we had forms consisting of one or two pages for listings, sales, counteroffers and earnest money receipts. The life of a real estate agent was fairly simple. Not so today. The number of forms (and the length of each) that one must fill out when listing and selling property increases every year. These are designed for the protection of seller, buyer and agent alike.

You must become totally familiar with every form used in your office. Get a sample set, read each form carefully and be sure you understand the meaning of each paragraph and what should be inserted in the blank spaces. Your sellers and buyers will often not understand various segments of the forms and you will be required to give explanations.

Practise taking a listing on a particular house, your own or that of a friend, and actually fill out the appropriate forms. Then pretend you have a buyer for that house and fill out an offer to purchase. In this way, you will more accurately pinpoint areas which you do not understand. Now is the time to make these discoveries, not when you are out in the field with a customer or client.

Make a list of all your questions and take them to your broker. Don't hesitate to ask again and again until you do understand; your license and your broker's license may depend upon the accuracy of your documentation. It is up to you to write it correctly. Seminars on contract writing are well worth attending, even for the seasoned agent.

4. Preview properties currently listed by associates in your office

Regardless of what area of sales you are in, be it automobiles, home appliances, clothing or real estate, you must know your product thoroughly before you can sell it to a customer. It is not enough to read the descriptions of your associates' listings on brochures, you need to tour them. Make a list of properties for sale in your office inventory, set up appointments and see as many of them as you can. Make good notes on your observations as discussed in Chapter 15.

5. Purchase up-to-date street maps of your city

You may be surprised at how often you will refer to these maps. Buy at least three copies: one for your desk at home, one for the office and a third for the glove compartment of your car. Licensees who are not familiar with the names and locations of all the streets in the area where they will be showing property should study the maps carefully. Even if you've lived a long time in your town, new streets and cul-de-sacs do appear.

6. Purchase "daytimer", etc.

To keep up with all the activities of a busy real estate agent, you must keep an appointment book (daytimer) current at all times. Choose a size that will fit into handbag, pocket, briefcase, glove compartment or wherever is most convenient for you to refer to it frequently. Some agents like to keep a second, desk-sized one as well.

More tools of the trade include a good calculator such as Texas Instruments' Business Analyst I or II, briefcase, 100' tape measure, and an answering machine for your home telephone. Useful items, too, are a tape deck for your car so that you can listen to real estate educational tapes, a micro tape recorder to record memos to yourself when away from the office and a contract phrase book.

You may not have the budget for it now but, once your career is rolling, a personal computer and a good word processing program can save you many hours of valuable time. When you do buy one, do so with the realization that you will have to make a time investment as well in order to learn how to utilize this tool.

7. Have photograph taken

It is my recommendation that you use your photograph on business cards, stationery, and for advertising and publicity.

Get a head-and-shoulders portrait taken by a professional and order black-and-white, 5"x7" glossy prints. Dress for the occasion with care, the hints in Chapter 4 will be helpful; ask the photographer's advice on colors which will enhance the picture (light shades are usually best) and explain that you want to convey an alert, friendly appearance.

8. Order business cards and stationery

Your broker may have an established account with a local printer from whom you should order your business cards and stationery. Obviously you will use the same format, style and color as fellow associates but all of them may not include a photograph. It costs a little more to do so but it's well worth it. Business cards are your cheapest form of advertising! Order a good supply. 500 is not too many for your first order and, since the cost to you per card decreases with larger orders, you may wish to consider getting 1,000.

9. Order name-riders and signs

As soon as you list your first house, you'll want to put your broker's for sale sign in the front yard. While it is customary for such signs to be provided by your office, it will most likely be up to you to provide your own name riders. This is a long, narrow plate which fits above or below the office sign and includes your name and home telephone number.

Again, your broker may have a preferred supplier for name riders. If not, look in the yellow pages of the telephone directory under "Signs" and you'll find a number of advertisements which indicate that real estate signs are made. Prices do vary so check several of them; quantity ordered effects cost so ask where the breaks occur. Six to ten is a good starting order for a new agent.

Some real estate offices maintain a supply of Open House signs and arrows; others expect associates to use their own. A large Open House sandwich board to place outside the home, plus ten to twelve arrows on stakes, will give you a good kit. Refer to Chapter 11 for more about the use of signs to help you decide the size of your order.

A Great Feeling Of Accomplishment

Wasn't that satisfying to cross off each of the items on this first "To Do" list as you executed them? It really is a simple, yet very effective, way to organize your life as a real estate agent. The habit will become second nature to you if you prepare a master set of "To Do" lists covering each stage of a real estate transaction as you finish the pertinent chapters in this book. You can then make photocopies from these masters to check off as you work your way through all the listings and sales you will be handling in the years ahead.

Be prepared for everything ...

2

Tell The World

We are in a "people service" business; if we want to be successful, we must do everything we can to make people aware that we are available.

Paid advertising in local newspapers is one way to announce your services but, perhaps surprisingly, it is not as effective as a free mention in the editorial columns. Try for the free mention first.

Your chance of gaining newspaper publicity depends upon a variety of circumstances. These may include such factors as editorial policy; space available (i.e. is "filler" material needed or are the columns tight because of a lot currently happening in the area), who you know at the paper, who you are and how professionally your material is prepared.

Check the pages of your daily newspaper to see which day of the week announcements of new business appointments usually appear; quite often you'll find them in the Sunday business section. There may be a notice on the page stating a deadline for submitting similar announcements; if not, phone the paper and ask for it. Ask, too, if you do not already know who it is, for the name of the editor of the business section.

If the newspaper has a special section for women, and you are a member of that sex, it may increase your chance of getting in print to send a second release to the women's editor. Try to think of a special angle for this one, i.e., "Jan Carpenter, past president of the Women's Auxiliary of St.

Francis Hospital, has just received her real estate license and has become associated with Home & Hearth Realty."

Besides dailies, prepare news releases for local weeklies as well; don't forget the publications of any clubs with which you are associated.

Writing The News Release

News releases should be typewritten in double spacing on 8.5"x11" paper. If your office letterhead is not this size, use plain paper with the office name and address typed at top left under the word "From". Use wide margins of at least one inch and drop down one-third of a page before starting the body of your text. Be sure your typewriter keys are clean and use a dark ribbon.

Editors cut news releases from the bottom. Put the "meat" of your story--your name and new affiliation--in the first paragraph. Give your background in the next paragraph or two. Keep the release short, no more than one page. A sample is presented on page 13.

When submitting your announcement to more than one daily newspaper, reword the first paragraph. This is not necessary for other intended recipients of the releases.

Do any of the publications on your list sometimes use photographs with announcements? If so, paperclip your news release to one of your new black-and-white glossy portraits. Type a caption consisting of your name and company name on a label (or piece of white paper) and attach it to the back. Never write on the back or front side of a photo or fold it in any way; damaged photos are not suitable for reproduction.

Proofread your news release and photo caption. Set it aside for a day, then read it again. Does it still impress you as being the best you can do? Is all spelling correct? Proofread it again.

Hand carry your news releases to the newspaper offices (or send by mail if this is incovenient) to the attention of the appropriate editor as soon as it is ready. Don't wait until deadline day.

Assuming your story gets into print, what results can you expect? It is still considered rather "special" to be in print and few who read the item will know that you provided it; the mention will give you a certain status. Friends who see it will call you and comment about your announcement. Acquaintances will be interested in what they read about you and may remember you are in real estate when they are next in the market to buy or sell. Strangers with whom you come in contact in the upcoming weeks may recognize your name from the newspaper item which will act as an ice-breaker in your dealings with them. You may receive calls from newcomers to town who need professional help to find housing and decided to contact you just because they read about you in the newspaper.

Paid Advertising

The advertising department of the newspaper can assist you with placement of a paid advertisement. Basically, you need to make three decisions: (a) size of space for the ad; (b) use of a photograph; (c) copy content.

Paid advertising costs usually depend upon the size of a newspaper's circulation; you can expect the rates to be lower for an ad in a local weekly than in the daily which generally offers a much wider readership. Budget may not permit you to use the daily but, even if you can afford the cost, consider if your money might not be better spent in the weekly. Most agents concentrate their efforts in a particular area so why buy coverage where you do not intend to do real estate business? If the weekly will reach the people you seek, you may be able to run the ad twice for what it will cost to have it appear once in the daily.

An ad of four to six "column inches" should be an adequate size for your announcement. One column inch represents a space that is one column wide and one inch in height; four column inches could either be one column wide by four inches high, or two columns wide by two inches high. This writer always advocates the use of your photograph and, for this reason, the two column format is preferred. If the pose in your photo is slightly turned in one direction or the other, be sure that you design the ad lay out so that the photo is turned towards the ad copy.

"Copy" refers to the words contained in the ad. For an announcement of your affiliation with Home & Hearth Realty, you will want to include your name, company name and address, telephone number of each and a message. A sample ad appears in Figure 3, page 22.

Home & Hearth Realty

12 State Street
Keston, CA 00000
Ph. (000) 000-0000

June 12, 1991

FOR IMMEDIATE RELEASE

Jan Carpenter has joined Home & Hearth Realty as a sales associate. Her appointment was announced today by William X. Pickerell, broker-owner of the ten-year-old company. She will be specializing in the sale of homes and condominiums in the Hazelwood Heights area.

A graduate of Keston High School and the University of California at San Diego, Mrs. Carpenter was previously an insurance adjustor with Smith & Pinkerton, Inc. She and her husband, Donald, a local stockbroker, have two children.

- end -

Figure I. Example of news release.

3

Tell Your Friends

*I*n the business of real estate, we earn commissions by selling property or by listing property that we or other agents sell. Most of us enjoy the variety offered by working in both listing and selling, but there are those who concentrate on one or the other. The latter will have you believe that their specialty is more challenging than the alternative. The truth is they have perfected the art of what they do so that their efforts reward them well.

When a seller decides to give up his present home, he plans, in one way or another, to change his lifestyle. He may have received an increase in income which enables him to move up to a bigger house or better neighborhood, or perhaps his children have grown to adulthood and left home so his housing needs have changed. Whatever the motivation, once the decision is made, he wants the transition to be quick and painless so that it interferes with his daily life as little as possible. Consequently, he will list with the real estate salesperson whom he believes has the greatest ability to help him accomplish his objectives.

You may well be that person, but how are you going to convince the seller? How are you even going to have a chance to try unless you know when he is getting ready to list? The first step is to make yourself known to an ever widening circle of people and the second is to make sure they never forget that you are a readily available real estate specialist.

There are three ways to accomplish these steps. One is by

means of "sphere-of-influence farming"; the second is via "geographic farming" and the third is through "demographic farming". Regardless of which type you are engaged in, you should make prospecting for clients an automatic part of your everyday routine. Set aside a minimum of thirty minutes each day by entering a prospecting slot in your daytimer. Keep this appointment with yourself just as you would if it involved a commitment with another person.

It is recommended that you begin real estate farming with the sphere-of-influence (SOI) method which will be discussed in this chapter. If you are a comparative newcomer to the area, you may find that the number of people on your SOI list will be limited and you will need to widen your pool of prospects by starting simultaneously with geographic farming (see Chapter 6).

Compile A List

Every person is at the center of a circle of their own acquaintances, friends and relatives. This circle is your "sphere-of-influence" and the people it embraces are prime prospects for business at this stage of your career. They should be the first ones told about your new career; mail a personal note to them when you take your news releases to the local newspapers. For many agents who fall by the wayside, this sphere encompasses both the beginning and ending of their tenure in real estate. If you follow the advice in this book, you will **not** be one of those casualties.

Have you ever thrown a pebble into a pond and watched as it became the hub of a widening circle of ripples? Perhaps your own sphere seems very small to you but you'll be amazed at how it grows as you work through the following steps in compiling your list of relatives, friends and acquaintances.

This sphere-of-influence list (SOI list) will be used a number of times so we will prepare it for easy use now and in future. Type the names and addresses (including zip codes) in three columns of eleven each on 8.5" x 11" sheets of paper. These pages will serve as your master list to photocopy onto sheets of self-adhesive labels each time you wish to send out mailings and for use in your record-keeping. The labels can be purchased in boxes of 100 or 250 sheets; each box includes a typing guide.

Compile your list from the following groups:

1.   Relatives of your own and your spouse who live in the general area;

2. Everyone in your current social circle;

3. Old friends whom you now see infrequently such as school and college friends who live in the area, people with whom you used to be on a bowling team or in a carpool, etc;

4. Neighbors as well as former neighbors who have moved to another part of town or nearby area;

5. Your acquaintances (people who at least know you by name). If you do not know their home addresses, look them up in either the telephone book or City Directory. Consider:

    Store clerks

    Bank tellers

    Mailperson

    Librarians

    Medical professionals (doctor, dentist, pharmacist, optometrist)

    Accountant

    Attorney

    Veterinarian

    Barber, hair stylist, manicurist

    Auto mechanic, service station personnel

6. Salesmen from whom you have purchased such items as car, truck, television, household appliances. Add those in service-related industries (travel, insurance, etc.)

7. Think back over your career history and add to your list the names of the people who would remember your name. For example:

    Former fellow employees, personnel directors, supervisors

    Customers/clients with whom you came in contact

    Employees of associated businesses, etc;

8. Are you a member of a local church, social clubs or groups such as political action, PTA, Lions, Toastmasters? Which members know you by name? Read through the membership directories to refresh your memory and add them to the list.* Get involved in the affairs of at least one of these concerns by volunteering to hold an office. A good position for a real estate agent is treasurer or the person responsible for mailing out the newsletter. You'll be among the first to find out who is planning to leave town and who are the newcomers.

9. Friends and fellow workers of your spouse who would recognize your name;

10. Parents of your children's friends.

The possibilities are endless. Once you start thinking about it, more and more acquaintances will pop into your mind. Keep a notepad handy and write the names down before you forget them again.

Write A Letter

Compose a letter to be mailed to your new SOI farm. Adapt the one suggested (Figure 2) to suit your needs or write one in your own words to announce your qualifications and readiness to assist whenever the recipient has real estate needs. Keep the following points in mind:

1. Do not put today's date on the letter. Instead, use the date on which you estimate you will actually be taking your mailing to the post office. Allow time for getting the letter reproduced and handsigned; addressing, stuffing, sealing and stamping envelopes; and, if being sent by bulk third class mail, sorted into zip code order.

2. The "Hello" salutation is used in the example. One alternative, if you have no relatives on your SOI list, is "Dear Friend". Another is to leave this line blank and, when you sign the printed letters, write in "Dear Mary and Jim", etc.

3. Too many of those people we would like to have as clients or customers do not realize all that we can do for them. They know that, as real estate agents, we should be contacted when they want to sell their home or

---

* The members with whom you are not yet acquainted can be included when you build a demographic farm (see page 45).

Home & Hearth Realty

12 State Street
Keston, CA 00000
Ph. (000) 000-0000

Jan Carpenter
Sales Associate
Home: (000) 000-0000

Date (**1**)

Hello: (2)

I have some good news which I want to share with you. Recently, I received my State license, and was proud to be invited to become an associate with Home & Hearth Realty, Keston's oldest and most successful real estate company.

A home of one's own has always been the American dream. This is why so many people are interested in what is happening in real estate. Those who do not own a home look forward to the day when they will be shopping for one; present homeowners enjoy seeing their equity build as neighborhood prices rise.

In my new career, I'm ready to help you with any aspect of real estate. Please telephone me when: (3)

(a) You have any questions concerning real estate.

(b) You notice a "For Sale" sign on a property anywhere in the area about which you would like details. It is immaterial whose sign it is. I will be glad to give you the information.

(c) You want to know the present market value of your home (either for information only or to consider selling). A complimentary market analysis is yours just for asking.

(d) You have friends or relatives moving to Keston. I would like to help them find a comfortable home.

Enclosed are several of my business cards for your convenience in contacting me. (4)

From time to time, I will be sending you news of real estate events in our town. Meanwhile when you "think real estate", please "think Jan Carpenter". I shall welcome the opportunity to be of service to you and your friends.

Your friend in real estate,

Jan Carpenter

Jan Carpenter
Sales Associate

P.S. - Your phone call is welcome, day or evening. My number at home is 000-0000. (5)

Figure 2. Sample letter to friends and acquaintances (sphere-of-influence). Numerals refer to points discussed on pages 17 and 19.

purchase another. Take this opportunity to specify other times when you would like to be of service:

A. Encourage members of your SOI list to get in touch with you whenever they have a real estate question. Don't be concerned about the possibility of not being able to answer their questions; if you don't know, you simply say you will get the information and call them back. The purpose is to train the members to turn to you for help on any subject related to real estate. The courteous and efficient manner in which you deal with their questions will influence their choice of a representative when they are ready to buy or sell.

B. It is important for people to understand the service that your membership in the multilist system enables you to provide for them. We are too inclined to take it for granted that the public knows we are not restricted to working only with the listings of our own company. Unfortunately, a large number, including personal friends, do not realize this fact.

C. When a family has plans to move to another area, it is natural to pass this news along to friends and/or business associates in that locale. This information is valuable to you so ask for it.

4. Business cards are your most inexpensive advertisement. Use them liberally. I would suggest enclosing a minimum of three cards with each of these letters. Some recipients may not even keep one; others will keep one for their own reference and pass the extras to others.

5. No, this writer did not forget to include this message in the body of the letter. It was deliberately placed as a postscript to attract attention. Those who receive your letter might read only one or two paragraphs of your letter but direct mail statistics indicate that most will read the postscript. It is a vital part of your composition; use one whenever you are sending out direct mail. In the body of the letter, we have asked the reader to telephone when we can be of help with real estate. The postscript emphasizes this point and indicates that we welcome calls at any time, even at home.

Incidentally, I learned the hard way not to count on the public understanding that MLS membership means that one agent can help them in connection with any home that is listed for sale. It is worth relating here in hopes that readers will benefit from my experience. I had been licensed about a year when I received a phone call from a close friend who was very excited and wanted to tell me her good news. Two years previously they had moved into a brand-new home and seemed very settled and happy. However, while on a Sunday afternoon drive in the country, they noticed a "For Sale" sign on a house which caught their fancy. Out of idle curiosity, they called the agent whose name was on the sign; she insisted upon showing it to them right away. She did her job very well; not only did she get their written offer to purchase that same afternoon but she also convinced them that, since the offer had to be contingent upon sale of their present home, she would be the best person to handle that as well! I asked my friend if she had tried to telephone me to show her the house before calling the listor; she said she could not do that because the house was listed with a different company. Needless to say, after that I made it crystal clear to everyone what a professional real estate salesperson with membership in the multiple listing service can do for them.

Reproducing Your Letter

Compose your draft with care, set it aside for one or two days, read it over with a fresh outlook to be sure it is still to your satisfaction. Type it in final form on white paper ready for reproduction. Read it through several times before you proceed to be sure that your letter is free of typing or spelling errors. You might even ask an associate to read it, too. It's amazing how easy it is to overlook mistakes at this stage but most of us spot them right away when they have been printed and it is too late!

The method for having your letter reproduced depends upon the extent of your budget and time as well as facilities available to you. If you're short on time and have a large budget, the best method is to turn everything over to a direct mail company. Look in the yellow pages of your telephone directory under such headings as "Advertising--Direct Mail", "Letter Shop Service" or "Mailing Lists". A typical state of newly-licensed agents is that they have more time than money so we'll work on this premise.

Some of today's copy machines are excellent and offer the least expensive way to handle the preparation of letters for direct mail. There may be a machine at your office and, in many towns, local copy shops now have good self-service machines. Be very critical about quality; use one which produces really sharp copies. Load the machine's tray with company letterhead and run off a sufficient number of letters to cover the names on your SOI list, one to mail to yourself, two file copies and several extras for people you may remember and add to the list by mailing date. Keep your original in case you need to make more copies of your letter later on.

If you do not have access to a good copier, you can have a professional copy shop or a print shop do the job. Generally the former are cheaper and faster. Telephone several and ask for quotations. State how many copies are required and advise that you will be providing camera-ready copy for reproduction on letterhead which you will provide.

Mechanics of Mailing

Use a copy machine to reproduce your typed list of names and addresses on to the self-adhesive labels. Make an extra set this first time for record keeping which we will discuss next chapter. Affix the labels and postage stamps to envelopes which have return address printed in upper left corner, sign your letters, fold (with business cards) and insert them into the envelopes.

Assuming that you have at least 200 names on your SOI list, you have a choice of mailing the letters by first class or third class. It has been my experience that local mail sent third class is often delivered as quickly as first class and I never hesitate to take advantage of the economical rate. In 1987, a first class stamp cost 22 cents as compared to 12.5 or less for a third class stamp.

Yes, the U.S. Postal Service does issue stamps for third class mail! They are sold in rolls of 500 and are so attractive that many people who casually glance at the front of the envelope before opening it do not realize that it did not travel first class. Never use the other third class system of having a preprinted postage paid square in the upper right hand corner of the envelope; this is an immediate red flag that it probably contains a piece of so-called "junk mail".

Before you can use the bulk mail system, a permit must be obtained; there is an application fee and annual renewal fee to be paid but, if you are going to be using the mails as much as you should, the savings are worthwhile. Before paying any fees, however, check to see if your office already has a permit.

U.S.P.S. has specific requirements for users of third-class mail to follow. Leaflets explaining in detail how to prepare your third-class mailing are available from U.S.P.S. and you shouid read them carefully. Letters have to be sorted into zip code order and bundied according to directions. Instead of being dropped into any mailbox, they must be handed in at the Post Office together with an applicable, completed form.

Be sure to include an envelope addressed to yourself so that you will know when the mailing is delivered. Its arrival is your "action alert" as you will discover in Chapter 5.

Getting Ready To Meet The Public

You have issued a news release and sent an announcement about your real estate services to your personal sphere-of-influence. Any day now you will be meeting potential buyers and sellers. First impressions are very important and you want yours to be favorable. In Chapter 4, we'll take a break from real estate matters and consider how you can put your best foot forward.

Home & Hearth Realty

(Head & shoulders photo of smiling agent who should be looking into ad copy or at the reader.)

is pleased to announce that

JAN   CARPENTER

has joined the staff at our
State Street   branch.

Jan has been an insurance adjustor in Keston for five years. She is a graduate of the University of California at San Diego. With Home & Hearth Realty, she will specialize in residential real estate. Whenever you have questions, or need help in buying or selling a home or condominium, please give Jan a call.

---

12 State Street ,   Keston, CA   Ph. (000) 000-0000

Figure 3. Example of paid advertisement (see page 12).

4

Put Your
Best Foot Forward

*P*eople in theatrical professions or creative fields tend to favor flamboyant attire; those who are offering a serious service for buyers and sellers of real estate will find a conservative dress approach more effective for them.

Suitable attire varies in different regions depending upon climate and the type of real estate one is selling. A man selling expensive homes in city and suburb would be wise to don suit and tie but his peer who specializes in ski condominiums would not look out of place on the job wearing parka, ski pants, sweater and boots. The agent who is showing residential property should avoid clothing which will compete with a home feature for buyers' attention; Mr. and Mrs. Buyer should be admiring the great fireplace in the family room, not looking at her form-fitting, red dress with its plunging neckline.

Further in this chapter there are separate sections for agents of opposite genders but, for now, let us consider wardrobe advice which applies to both.

When women shop for shoes, style is usually foremost in their minds. In my opinion, although style is a factor, the prime requisite for both men and women to seek is a combination of both comfort and style. A real estate agent spends a lot of time standing, walking and climbing stairs. By the end of the day, aching feet will have a detrimental effect on your disposition and could ruin your chances of closing a deal.

Leather, kept clean and polished, is the best material for looks, durability and easy care. For men, lace-up or slip-on shoes (not loafers) in black or dark brown offer a businesslike appearance and, when not being worn, should should have shoetrees slipped inside. Best for women are leather pumps with medium heel (no more than two inches) which can, in appropriate seasons, be of open-toed and/or sling back style. Owning a pair in each of the basic black, brown and gray shades, with beige and white for summer, gives you year-round versatility.

A cardigan sweater is a useful item for men and women. Cashmere, mohair or wool Arans are very suitable. (Nice selections of these are found, incidentally, in two free mail order catalogs published by Shannon Mail Order, Shannon Free Airport, Ireland, and Cashs, P.O. Box 47, St. Patrick Street, Cork, Ireland.)

Pockets are desirable in a cardigan and other clothing items. They provide a place to keep a few business cards handy and 3"x5" cards to remind you to cover certain items. If you have the distracting habit of waving your hands around when speaking, or never know what to do with them, you can simply tuck them in the pockets. Many of us will take out a pen, use it and then absentmindedly click it as we carry it around; put the pen in a pocket instead.

A good raincoat is almost a necessity in many areas and, with a zip-out lining, can double as a winter coat for those on a limited budget. Years ago, our British cousins set a smart style trend with the Burberry; this has endured and never seems to lose its popularity. Preferred colors for both sexes are the versatile beiges and tans.

Tips For Women In Real Estate

A recommended wardrobe for a female agent would include these clothing items in both winter and summer weights:

> Blazers
> Raincoat
> Full-length coat
> Suits
> Skirts
> Blouses in long and short sleeves
> Shirtwaist and other style dresses
> Cardigan sweater
> Several pairs of shoes and boots
> Leather handbags, briefcase, umbrella.

Your wardrobe will seem more extensive when you mix and match blouses, skirts and blazers so choose them in compatible colors. Avoid material designed with loud prints and select feminine, but not fussy, designs. As you try on skirts and dresses in the shops, look in the mirror to observe the length and way in which they hang during a sitting and standing test. You do not want to find yourself putting on an impromptu leg display while driving Mr. and Mrs. Buyer to see homes, or while bending over to inspect a floor crack during a listing tour guided by Mr. Seller. Slacks and the once popular pantsuits (not jeans) may still be worn by agents during winters in very cold climate regions but dresses and skirts are always better choices otherwise.

Accessories

Real estate agents always have a lot to carry around: pocket calculator, pen, pencil, measure, notebook, map, etc. It makes sense to keep them in a briefcase but many of us are lost without a handbag. Both, when used together, are too much. Either select roomy handbags with shoulder straps or carry your briefcase and keep cosmetic and other personal items in a small holder inside.

Take care not to wear distracting accessories. Choose belts, gloves and scarves that compliment, not compete with, your outfit. A highnecked dress can be enhanced with a row of pearls or a gold or silver plain necklace. If you must wear earrings, avoid the type which dangle. In general, try to limit jewelry on the job to a slim wristwatch, wedding and/or engagement ring(s) and the N.A.R. pin.

Grooming

Good grooming is essential for a successful real estate agent. Keep your nails neatly trimmed, filed and buffed; long talons may look good on a model but might set Mr. Buyer's teeth on edge as you write up his offer to purchase a home. Before deciding to use nail polish, realize that this requires more upkeep time. Nails sporting last week's chipped and peeling polish are most unattractive. Polish, of course, should be restricted to natural, pearl or soft pinks.

Choose a hair style that is easy for you to keep neat; bangs which cover up half your eyes, or a peek-a-boo look which covers one eye most of the time, will make it difficult for you to maintain eye-contact with your customers and clients. Length is a matter of personal preference but, if you have long hair, wear it up on the job. Professional advice with styling can be invaluable and a hairdresser who is skilled with the scissors is a jewel. If you do not already have someone really good, observe other agents at meetings and notice those whose hair is always attractive in its appearance; ask each of them who does their hair.

Hair should be washed at least three times each week using a good shampoo and conditioner. When doing it yourself, try to schedule shampoos when you expect to be working at home and allow your hair to air dry; heat appliances used frequently tend to damage hair.

Many department stores offer free cosmetic advice, demonstrations on makeup application and have samples of products for customers to try. Spend some time talking to the clerks and experimenting with different brands and types to find which are best suited to you. In general, it is best to aspire to the natural look and avoid any hint of garishness in vivid shades of lipstick or eyeshadow.

Tips For Men In Real Estate

The basic wardrobe for men pursuing a career in real estate should include:

> Business suits
> Button-down and regular collar shirts
> Five silk ties in quiet designs, i.e. diagonal
>   stripes; small, subdued geometric pattern or
>   pinpoint dots
> Solid color blazers
> Trousers (preferably solid colors)
> Topcoat and/or raincoat
> Leather shoes and belts
> Briefcase, umbrella

The number of suits needed will vary according to climate. If it is similar year-round, four or five will do nicely; otherwise, the number will have to almost double to allow for suits in lightweight materials for summer wear and in heavier wools for winters. Since well-cut suits are expensive, stay with classic styles rather than current fashions and take the time when shopping to be sure that the suit, especially the jacket, fits well. Two-button, single-breasted jackets are the most convenient. Solid colors (the tans, grays, medium blues, navy) are best but a subtle, narrow pinstripe is good for variation. Black suits are really too formal for real estate and dark brown is a difficult color for a lot of people to wear.

Choose your blazers and trousers with the thought in mind of being able to wear any one of the blazers with any pair of the trousers. Stay with solid colors for the trousers and generally for the blazers, too, but a tweed or herringbone is acceptable if the style is not too casual. Cuffless trousers are preferred and, please, keep your billfold out of the back pocket! Even in your inside jacket pocket it will result in a bulge if you do not make it a habit to purge its contents regularly and limit them to the minimum necessities.

Long-sleeved shirts are recommended for the real estate professional with unusually hot climate being the only excuse to wear short sleeves on the job. Shirts in whites and pale pastel shades of blue or beige will compliment your suits and blazers. Laundry preference will influence the material you choose; a cotton wardrobe goes to the corner laundry while the polyester blends, touched up with an iron, emerge fairly well from your efforts at home. Advantages to using the corner laundry, apart from the fact that their service will give you a better appearance, include the value of regular contact with owner and/or clerks and the opportunity to learn about their customers' real estate needs.

Jewelry is best set aside for social occasions but a good quality wristwatch, wedding band or signet ring and the N.A.R. pin are certainly very acceptable on the job.

Should you grow a mustache, long sideburns or a beard? No! Be clean-shaven and, if necessary, shave twice daily; an electric razor is a useful item to keep at the office or in your car for unexpected afternoon appointments. Choose a simple hairstyle and visit your barber or stylist regularly every third or fourth week to maintain a neat appearance. Shampoo your hair daily or, at the minimum, three to four times each week.

Diet, Weight Control, Exercise & Personal Hygiene

Real estate is a demanding career both mentally and physically and it is much easier to avoid stress when one is in excellent health. It is my suggestion that every new agent arrange to have both a physical and dental check up before the first day on the job.

Those among us who are overweight should ask themselves, do I really want to carry those extra pounds up and down the thousands of stairs I will be traversing in the coming months? Of course not! This is a good time to follow a doctor-recommended program of diet and exercise and lose them. Besides, think how much better you will look in your real estate wardrobe and how much your self-esteem will increase.

We get so busy during the day that it is easy to postpone daily exercise. Or we may think we get enough of it while showing homes. Exercise is something that everyone needs not just those who are trying to lose weight; once you get into the habit, you will find that it provides a welcome break. Block out a daily exercise period in your appointment book and spend the time walking, running, jogging, bicycling, swimming, doing aerobics, playing raquetball or tennis, etc. Attach to this appointment the same degree of importance you would if it was one to have lunch with a prospect; do not regard it as merely something that you'll do if you feel like it and the weather is nice or nothing else comes up. If you feel guilty about taking this time for yourself (you should not), make a point of finding out the favorite exercise activities of members of your farm(s) and make appointments with different ones so that you can combine your daily exercise break with business!

It's very easy to skip meals or to eat a lot of fast-food because we just get too busy to take time out. An improperly fuelled furnace doesn't do a very good job heating the house, nor will your nutrient-deprived body and brain work as efficiently on the job. Consult your doctor for diet advice, or read some of the good books written on this subject.

We spend a great deal of time cultivating prospects. Once we have them in our corner, we must continue to please them not only professionally but with our appearance so a few reminders concerning personal hygiene are appropriate. Remember to use a deodorant/antiperspirant product after your morning ablutions and why not have a small toothbrush and paste with you so that you can brush your teeth whenever you eat? Particles of food remaining in your mouth (from snacks as well as meals) can result in unpleasant breath of which you may not be aware but will be noticed by those with whom you converse. See your dentist annually for a checkup and professional cleaning.

If you are a smoker of cigarettes, pipe or cigars, never smoke around customers or clients (even if they do) or in an Open House between visitors. Keep a breath freshening spray handy and use it regularly each time you have smoked.

Your Automobile

When you see your peers driving around in big expensive cars, it is only natural to envy their success. We, and most likely sellers and buyers, too, just assume that they are successful because they can afford to drive these cars. We never stop to consider that their equity may be very small, the cars could even be leased, and they really have to struggle to come up with the monthly payment. Perhaps you've already heard the story about the new agent whose broker took him to the local Cadillac dealer on his first day at work and told him to pick out the one he wanted. The broker had no intention of buying it for him, he merely wanted to be sure the salesman would go out and do whatever it took to sell real estate; those big payments would provide a "driving" incentive!

This premise is not without merit. In my mid-twenties, I had just forsaken the security of a full-time newspaper job to become a freelance writer when my old car called it quits. My budget said "no", but my heart said "yes" so the bank and I bought a brand new convertible. Much to my surprise, that car brought me a lot of well-paid assignments from advertising agencies which I would never have been given had I been driving around town in my old clunker. It was an advance symbol of a success which I had not yet earned and it made me very determined that it would not go back to the dealer through any fault of mine.

Although I do believe in the psychological value to an agent of driving an impressive car, I do not feel that a new agent should have to acquire an expensive, current model fresh off the showroom floor in order to do well in real estate. What I do believe is that it is necessary to have a presentable, smooth-running, dependable automobile which is kept scrupulously clean both inside and out.

Keep in mind, too, that a new car smells really good and so should yours, regardless of its vintage. The favorite perfume of a woman in real estate (after-shave lotion or cologne in the case of a man) may be offensive to a customer who is a passenger in the confines of your car. If you are a smoker, try to restrain yourself from ever smoking in your real estate car whether with customers or not. Non-smokers have a very keen sense of smell and will not appreciate inhaling a stale odor which, unfortunately, lingers a very long time. You probably won't notice it, but your customers will.

Ask your insurance agent if the coverage you already have is adequate for your occupation as a real estate salesperson. When you will be driving customers in your car, check the gas tank before picking them up so that you don't have to stop to refuel while they are with you.

5

People Pursuit

*N*ow that we've given thought to ways in which to make a good personal impression when meeting potential buyers and sellers, let's get back to the letters in Chapter 3 which are now en route to your friends and acquaintances. What do you do while waiting for their reactions? You start work on the next stage of making things happen! To be successful in real estate, you must learn to be adept at people pursuit. The more people you talk to about real estate, the larger your business will grow.

Keeping Records

The compilation of your list and the mailing you have just completed are actually the first steps in "sphere-of-influence farming". You have chosen your acres and planted the initial crop. To gain the best harvest, it is important to keep records of everything you do. The busier you get the harder it will be to remember all the details of your contacts with specific people. Get in the habit now of writing everything down.

While USPS is delivering your letters, set up a record system either on file cards (4"x6" or 5"x8") or on sheets in a 3-ring binder. For now, we will assume that you decide to use 5"x8" cards. You will also need a box in which to file the cards. I recommend the cabinet type; boxes with lids are more economical but, if you drop the box, you'll have all your cards to pick up and sort out.

It is time-saving to have a form printed on the cards such

as the one shown in Figure 4. Allot a card to each person in your SOI farm and affix a label in the top right hand corner peeled from the second label set of your master list. File the cards in the drawer between alphabetical dividers.

Whenever you have any type of contact with a member of your SOI farm, summarize the details on the appropriate card. Each time you intend to contact such a person, first refer to the card to remind yourself what has previously transpired. The only exception is when you send out a general mailing to everyone. A record of general contacts should be kept on a separate card such as the example shown in Figure 5 on page 37; at least two copies of the letter, card or other item mailed should be retained for future reference in a file folder.

```
╔══════════════════════════════════════════════════╗
║       S-O-I   MEMBER   RECORD   CARD               ║
║  HOME PHONE           ┌──────────────────────────┐ ║
║  BUSINESS PHONE       │   Affix name-address      │ ║
║                       │   label here.             │ ║
║  RENTS      HOMEOWNER └──────────────────────────┘ ║
║  BIRTHDAY/OTHER IMPORTANT DATES                    ║
║  FAMILY                                            ║
║  REAL ESTATE INTERESTS/NEEDS                       ║
║ ─────────┬────────┬─────────┬─────────────────────║
║ Contact  │ Method │ Purpose │  Response/Comments   ║
║ date     │        │         │                      ║
║          │        │         │                      ║
║          │        │         │                      ║
║          │        │         │                      ║
║          │        │         │                      ║
║          │        │         │    ASK  FOR  LEADS!  ║
╚══════════════════════════════════════════════════╝
```

Figure 4. Record card for member of a sphere-of-influence farm. When the person is a homeowner, enter details on back of card.

Response To Your Letters

Since the people on your SOI mailing list are comprised of those who are known to you in varying degrees from slight acquaintance through close relatives, you will receive comments during the days and weeks after the letters are received. You might get some telephone calls, congratulations from those you meet, and even a few written notes with best wishes for your future. These are all very nice but it's up to you to get the most mileage out of these friendly overtures.

When offered congratulations in person or over the telephone,

Don't say: "Thank you. I think I'll enjoy it. How's your wife?"

Say: "Thank you, Bob. I'm really anxious to get started. Do you happen to know anyone who is thinking about buying or selling real estate?"

Bob may or may not be able to give you a lead that day. Be sure to insert into your conversation that you would appreciate his letting you know anytime he does hear of anyone thinking along those lines. It is important for your contacts to be gently educated that although it is great when they recommend your services to another party, you do need to be advised of that party's interest in real estate as well. This gives you the opportunity to contact the third party direct and avoid the risk of hesitancy or forgetfulness in getting in touch with you.

Answer any notes that you receive with a phone call of appreciation. Again, ask for leads.

Make a notation about all responses received on the appropriate record cards and put them back in the box together behind a "Responded" divider.

Non-Response

Counting from the day your self-addressed "action alert" letter reaches you, allow one week for voluntary response, then initiate follow up contacting of the people you have not heard from. To do this, make up five file dividers in your record box, one for each respective day Monday through Friday, and evenly divide between them the cards for the people from whom you have not heard. The number of people you will contact daily has to be determined by time available but you should try to complete the task in two to three weeks.

Once you identify yourself on the phone to these SOI people, it is quite possible that a number of them will mention your letter themselves.

> **Say:** "That's why I was calling this morning. I'm anxious to get started and wondered if you happen to know anyone who is thinking about buying or selling real estate?"

In the case of the ones who do not bring up the subject of your new career, after you've dispensed with the preliminary how-are-you's, proceed:

> "I sent you a letter recently about my new career in real estate. I'm really anxious to get started and wanted to ask you if you know anyone who is considering moving this year?"

Variations on the "I'm anxious to get started" line are, "I'm looking forward to being of service"; or "I'm now building a customer/client list". Use the one best suited to the particular person you are addressing.

Do you know the definition of the terms "customer" and "client"? In most cases, the client is the seller of a listed property and the customer is the buyer. An exception occurs when you are acting as "buyer's broker" and the buyer is the person who will pay for services rendered.

Obviously it is very possible that there will be a number of persons in your SOI farm who may misinterpret your request for leads. They may feel they are being asked to recommend your service, without having personally experienced it, to a friend or business associate who they know is about to buy or sell real estate. Poor representation by you could reflect on them so it is easier to deny you the lead than gamble on your capabilities. Help them to put such qualms aside by saying:

> "Naturally, I am not asking you to personally recommend me to act as agent. What I would appreciate is having the name of anyone you know who may be thinking of buying or selling. I will then contact them with information about my company's services and explain how we can help."

As you complete each call, write a comment on the record card and refile it with the alphabetical dividers. When all calls have been made, preferably within two to three weeks, refile all cards, including the ones for those people who did respond, into the alphabetical dividers in readiness for the next phase of the program.

Continued Cultivation

Busy people have short memories. Farm fields need constant attention for best results and you must touch bases with your SOI farm members on a regular basis.

Each person should receive about six phone calls from you during the year. Put the months of the year on file card dividers and insert the ones for the upcoming two months into your alphabetical box with the record cards divided between them. Assuming you are starting at the beginning of a year, head the first section with the JANUARY divider and the second with FEBRUARY.

During the month of January, phone the people listed on those cards. Set yourself a minimum daily quota by using your Monday through Friday dividers to spread the task evenly through the month. Establish a format to follow in each conversation such as the following:

1. Identify yourself by name and company, i.e., "This is Jan Carpenter, Home & Hearth Realty. How are you?" Engage in preliminary small talk to establish rapport but keep it as brief as possible to conserve both your own time and that of the person called as well.

2. Follow up applicable data noted on the person's card if there is anything pertinent.

3. Give the person some real estate news such as lowered interest rates, a new development to be constructed in the area, etc. Most interesting to your listeners would be details of a new listing or sale in the street where they reside. Before dialling, look in the MLS records for recent activity as this is a very good item to bring into the conversation. It shows you are alert to current real estate events which interest them and is a natural lead to the question, "Are you having any thoughts about making a move yourself?"

4. Ask if the person has any question or problem with which you might be able to help concerning real estate. In the event you are asked something you cannot answer, don't try to guess. Admit that you don't know and say you will find out and will call back as soon as possible with the

information.

5. Ask if the person knows of anyone who is thinking of buying or selling real estate.

Jot down on each card the pertinent data gleaned from your conversation then, if no further action (such as obtaining information or follow-up of a lead furnished) is required, file it behind the March divider. In February, call the people on that month's cards and move them back behind the April divider.

When a conversation leads to third party sellers or buyers or requests for information, file those cards behind an "Action Pending" divider. Check through this section every day and handle the requirements as quickly as possible. If you have been given a lead, write a thank you note for same and say you will advise the outcome. Contact the potential seller/buyer and offer your services (see chapters 9 or 14). Once the required action has been completed, remember to remove the card from "Action Pending" and refile in the section for that month in which next phone call is to be made.

Making The Most Of Mealtime

It is customary for most people to take time out for beverage and lunch breaks. You can spend this time alone, while it away with an office associate, or you can put it to productive use. Plan your week's breaks to be spent in the company of selected members of your sphere-of-influence farm.

Initially you will have to rely on your judgment as to which ones are most likely to be the best contacts for real estate business either on their own account or by giving you referrals. You might start with the ones who could logically be expected to know the most number of people such as professional businesspersons, barber and beauty shop operators, club secretaries, active members of local churches, etc. Later, your mailing and telephone program will give you indications of which persons you should cultivate in this manner.

Consider joining one or more community clubs which have weekly breakfast meetings. You'll meet new prospects and will be able to add to your SOI list. Many of these clubs have membership lists available to other members; even the ones you never meet personally can be used in demographic farming with an initial letter mentioning your common bond of membership in that club.

More Mail Contact

In between telephone contacts, keep your name and occupation alive in the minds of your SOI farm members by mail contact. Do this in an organized manner by working out your program now, writing it down in your daytimer and pursuing it in a timely manner. Your program for one-half of your farm (we'll refer to it as Section A) might resemble the following plan in which the starting month happens to be January:

Month 1	(Jan.)	Letter
Month 2	(Feb.)	Telephone call
Month 3	(Mar.)	Greeting card (St. Patrick's Day or Easter)
Month 4	(Apr.)	Telephone call
Month 5	(May)	Letter
Month 6	(June)	Telephone call
Month 7	(July)	Greeting card (Independence Day)
Month 8	(Aug.)	Telephone call
Month 9	(Sept.)	Letter
Month 10	(Oct.)	Telephone call
Month 11	(Nov.)	Thanksgiving Day card
Month 12	(Dec.)	Season's greetings by card, letter or phone.

Reverse the order of the program for people in Section B, the second half of your farm, so that they receive a phone call in January and a letter in February.

Greeting cards are good attention-getters. One reasonably-priced source for them is Current, Inc., Colorado Springs, CO 80941. Handwrite a brief message and enclose two of your business cards. Try to discover dates of special occasions in the lives of your farm members and note them on the record cards; birthday and anniversary cards are always appreciated. During conversations with your people, if vacation plans are mentioned, note the date and send a "happy vacation" card. Never overlook an opportunity to remind your prospects of your existence.

Handle the letters in the same manner as previously described. Greeting cards, too, can be sent by third class mail but, if one-half of your overall farm does not total 200, you will have to use first-class mail for both letters and cards. When you expand into geographic or demographic farming, you may be able to time your mailings to go out concurrently and the number will qualify for the lower rate provided that the size and weight of each piece is the same.

Remember to add to your SOI farm the names of new people you meet in the course of your everyday life. All of its members know who you are. You're over the first hurdle in winning their trust. Now let's learn how to make friends of strangers.

SPHERE-OF-INFLUENCE MAILING RECORD

Mailing date	Type	Section & No.	Total cost	Response

Figure 5.   Record of general mailings sent to members of a sphere-of-influence farm.   Date of mailing should be written in first column. In the second, enter type of mailing, i.e. letter, postcard, greeting card (note occasion). Indicate the farm section which received this mailing in the third column together with number sent.   Record the total mailing cost in the fourth one including materials, printing/photocopying, mailing service (if used) and postage.   In the Response column, show a summary only of the results attained after a suitable time lapse to allow full impact and follow up, i.e. one listing (Berg), two referrals (Matson, Davis). Although general mailings are not entered on individual record cards, responses received do need to be detailed on the appropriate members' cards.

6

Geographic Farming

We accomplish two useful purposes by establishing a geographic farm. Not only do we widen our circle of friends and acquaintances, but we become a specialist in a particular neighborhood as well. The most successful people in real estate are either farmers now or got their start in this manner.

The ideal and easy way to get off to a fast start would be to buy an already-established geographic farm. You would gain the benefit of immediate access to the seller's records including a complete history of the farm, its operation, occupant data, results attained, etc. Further, the farm's seller might be willing to personally introduce you to its residents which is the best possible way to become acquainted with them.

Unfortunately, established farms are not readily available or advertised. It is surprising that the person who has farmed successfully over a period of years and, perhaps because of retirement or other reason, is no longer going to be working the farm, seldom realizes that he/she is walking away from a valuable asset and actually has a piece of desirable, intangible property to offer for sale.

Your broker may be able to put you in touch with a former farmer, or one who is about to retire. Perhaps there is a "Haves & Wants" sheet circulated among the local real estate community in which you could advertise your interest in acquiring an existing farm. It should be realized, of course, that the purchase of someone else's farm carries no guarantee of an exclusive territory or the same degree of success that the seller enjoyed. You would be buying an opportunity; it would be up to you to make your own success by means of your knowledge, diligence and quality of service provided.

Organizing A Geographic Farm

Choose a neighborhood for your farm that is at least two years old. A newly-built housing area will not be productive. Some agents feel at home farming the area where they live; others prefer to farm elsewhere so as to keep their personal and professional lives separated.

Real estate is a numbers game. The more territory you cover, the better your chance of getting business; however, do not start with more homes than you can comfortably service. After you have read this chapter, you will realize that geographic farming makes great demands upon your time so it should be no larger than you can operate efficiently. A minimum of 200 homes is suggested as a starting number, later you may want to expand to as many as 500. It is not necessary to match the size of your farm with that of the entire subdivision; begin with a portion of it and, if you find you can handle more, add extra homes as you go along.

Prepare a list of the subdivision's resident-owners from County records or ask for assistance from a title company. Set up a farm book in a 3-ring binder with a page for each home (or use a card system). Some farmers now like to maintain these records on a computer. Study old multilist catalogs to become thoroughly familiar with homes in the farm and their past market activity. Enter the data in your records. If your farm is a condominium complex rather than an area of houses, obtain and peruse copies of the by-laws and declarations (see Chapter 20).

Contacting Farm Residents

The first task of a new farmer is to become acquainted with everyone who lives in the farm. Before you can expect to list a home, you must impress its owner with your capabilities. A well-planned contact program consisting of regular mailings, telephone calls and door-to-door visits will enable you to do these things. It should be mentioned that there are a few areas in the United States where local laws forbid door-to-door prospecting.

Your contact program should be handled on a regular basis, not spasmodically when you feel in the mood to do it.

Self-discipline and perseverance are attributes that the farmer must adopt.

Plan your farming contact program annually for the year ahead. It might look like this:

1st month	Letter of introduction
2nd month	Mail plus door-to-door visiting
3rd month	Mail. Telephone call
4th month	Mail
5th month	Mail. Door-to-door
6th month	Mail. Telephone call
7th month	Mail. Door-to-door
8th month	Mail. Telephone call
9th month	Mail. Door-to-door
10th month	Mail. Telephone call
11tn month	Mail
12th month	Mail

Mail, in my opinion, is the easiest and least expensive method to keep your name and service fresh in the minds of your prospects. The above campaign uses mail every month, even in the months when telephone or door-to-door contacting is also suggested. You may miss some of your farm residents during personal visits or telephone calling, but the mail will always reach them. In Figure 6, a typical introductory letter is presented. It is not necessary to write a letter every month; substitute a greeting card occasionally for variety. Your enclosed business card is a subtle reminder that you are ready to assist with the recipients' real estate needs. Another alternative is the circulation of a neighborhood newsletter or advertising bulletin.

Make careful notes of any information gathered during telephone and door-to-door contacting. These notes should not

Home & Hearth Realty

12 State Street
Keston, CA 00000
Ph. (000) 000-0000

Jan Carpenter
Sales Associate
Home: (000) 000-0000

January 11, 1991

Dear Neighbor:

Just a note to let you know that Bill Pickerell, broker-owner of Home & Hearth Realty, has appointed me as the company's representative in Hazelwood Heights. Since I live here myself, I am really pleased about this and welcome the opportunity to be of service to you and my other neighbors.

In the coming months, via letters, telephone calls and personal visits, I plan to keep you up-to-date with real estate happenings in Keston. I'm ready to help you with any aspect of real estate. Please telephone me when:

1. *You have any questions concerning real estate.*

2. *You notice a "For Sale" sign on a property anywhere in the area about which you would like details. I will be glad to give you complete information no matter whose sign is in the yard.*

3. *You want to know the present market value of your home (either for information only or to consider selling). A complimentary market analysis is yours just for asking.*

4. *You have friends or relatives moving to Keston. I would like to help them find the right home and make their transition as smooth as possible.*

- 1 -

Figure 6. Example of letter to residents of a geographic farm.

- 2 -

Home & Hearth Realty's broker, Bill Pickerell, started the company ten years ago. In 1979, he organized Keston's first Pumpkin Parade which, as you know, is a popular (and growing) annual event on State Street. He was also responsible for starting "Caretaker Watch" in several local neighborhoods, including Hazelwood Heights; the program has resulted in a gratifying lowering of crime statistics. Twenty full-time agents now work in our State Street office and we are all proud of Home & Hearth's reputation for service and community spirit.

On a personal level, I am a graduate of Keston High School and the University of California at San Diego. A number of you already know that, for the past five years, I have worked as an insurance adjustor with Smith & Pinkerton. I am now enjoying the challenge of my new role in real estate as sales associate with Home & Hearth Realty.

I look forward to seeing you very soon.

Your Hazelwood Heights neighbor,

Jan Carpenter
Sales Associate

P.S. - Enclosed are several of my business cards for your convenience in contacting me. You will find both my home and office numbers and you are welcome to call me at any time, day or evening.

Note: If your home is now listed for sale with another broker, please disregard this letter. It is not my intent to solicit the listings of other real estate brokers.

only cover real estate related comments made by homeowners but also data about their personal lives. For example, listen for hints which will reveal the important dates in their lives (family birthdays, anniversaries); how they spend their vacations; hobbies; names of pets they own, etc. You can use this material to your advantage in establishing good rapport. As we grow older, the number of cards in the mail on our birthday lessens; your card will merit attention. Try to fix their faces in your memory so that you will be able to recognize and greet these people by name when you meet them on the street or in stores. Asking how the family enjoyed their vacation in Mexico, or if Fluffy, the family cat, has had her kittens, will show them that you are alert and interested in their lives. You will be remembered when such people are ready to sell or buy real estate and need professional assistance.

Scheduled door-to-door visiting is limited to four per year in the plan outlined. Going door-to-door is the most time-consuming method of contact but even today it can prove productive. Years ago, going door-to-door gave the salesperson a good opportunity to visit with the lady of the house. In a special report for "Reader's Digest" by Carl T. Rowan and David M. Mazie (June, 1985), it was revealed that over two-thirds of American women with school-age children worked outside their homes in 1984. If this statistic holds true in a 300-home farm, you would only find one hundred housewives at home. Obviously, then, you are going to have to determine as early in your farming as you can which homes are occupied during the day and which are not. You can then time your visits so that they will be made when the residents are at home which will mean early evening and Saturday calling (never on Sunday, please).

You will note that the outline calls for your first visit to be made in your second farming month. This face-to-face contact is a good follow up to your introductory letter. Keep this visit brief, be friendly and again emphasize your desire to be of service. The next two visits on the outline are shown in the fifth and seventh months and are intended to coincide with the start and middle of the summer season. Summer is the prime marketing time for homes so, when you plan your own schedule, arrange door-to-door contacting accordingly with immediate new listings as your objective. The final visit for the year is made in September, the ninth month on the outline; this timing could afford you a chance to pick up homes that were listed with other companies and expired without sale.

Have butterflies in your tummy when its time for your first door-to-door visits? Probably the worst that can happen to you is that a rude owner will slam the door in your face. Most people are basically polite and you will seldom experience such treatment. Besides you are not a total stranger, you have already introduced yourself by mail.

To give yourself further encouragement, consider the positive effect your visits can have on your income. Assume that you knock on fifty doors and get one lead which results in a listing. It subsequently sells for $85,000 through another broker's office. The commission negotiated with the seller was 6%, half of which your broker paid to the cooperating broker. You, as listing agent on a 60/40 split, are paid $1,020. What does this indicate? Each one of the 49 negative responses you heard was akin to putting $20.81 into your bank account. So, as you go on your rounds looking for a listing, mentally pay yourself $20.81 each time you hear "no" and enjoy watching the total grow en route to "yes".

Outgoing Telephone Calls

Telephone prospecting requires initial courage. Once you have made a few, your apprehensions will evaporate. With fifty to one hundred behind you and results apparent, you'll feel like an old pro and wonder why you didn't prospect this way sooner.

The same rules apply here as when you answer the phone (see Chapter 13). Above all else, smile; don't allow your voice to frown. When your call is answered, identify yourself and convey your reason for telephoning. As your conversation moves along, and it will flow very smoothly if you have learned something about the household and its interests, you can inquire if the owner has any friends or knows of anyone in the neighborhood who is thinking about selling. Of course, you would never call and ask if the owner is interested in selling the house---that's a sure way to get a quick "No. Goodbye."

Telephone calling is a good companion for direct mail. It gives you a chance to follow up on letters, chat briefly with each homeowner and ask specifically about real estate related affairs. Avoid calling at mealtimes or when a popular television program is being aired.

Further Reading

Geographic farming is a surefire method to reap big rewards in your real estate career but the subject is too complex for a few pages. It is covered in great detail in a book by this writer entitled "Real Estate Farming: Campaign For $uccess" (Kricket Publications, P.O. Box 91832, Santa Barbara, CA 93190).

More Farming Opportunities

Demographic farming is another way to find prospects for real estate business. Its members are composed of people who share something in common; they may, for example, be members of the same profession (attorneys, doctors, dentists, accountants), attend the same church, or belong to a particular athletic or social club. If you made up groups of prospects consisting of apartment dwellers or newlyweds, again you would be building demographic farms.

Typical sources for names would be the yellow pages of telephone directories; church or club membership rosters; or lists purchased from mailing brokers. "Direct Mail List Rates & Data" is a national directory of lists offered by brokers; it is issued regularly by Standard Rate & Data Publishing Company and your local library may have a copy. Follow up newspaper announcements of births, deaths, engagements, weddings, promotions and transfers because they are often signals of a pending change in present housing style and, as such, another source of names.

A demographic farm should be set up and operated in a similar manner to the sphere-of-influence farm.

7

For Sale By Owner

$\mathcal{P}$ity the poor person who decides to sell his home himself. As soon as his FSBO sign appears in his front yard and his advertisement starts to run in the local newspaper, his phone will ring and people will beat a path to his door. Why feel sorry for a seller whose advertising is generating such lively action? These are not would-be buyers inquiring about the home, these are your fellow real estate agents trying to list the home for sale! It is obvious that your own prospecting methods must be very well planned and executed so that you are the one who is successful.

Philosophy Of A FSBO

Cultivating the FSBO is yet another form of farming but the time element is completely different from the more leisurely approach of the varieties we've talked about so far. Previously we have been ploughing and tilling selected fields, planting seeds and giving them regular attention as we wait patiently for them to sprout. Now we are confronted with full-grown plants that have suddenly sprung up with no loving care from us and which are subject to harvesting by absolutely anyone who happens along at the moment the fruit is ripe for picking. We want that person to be us.

Before we review the best way to approach this situation, we should first try to understand the philosophy of Mr. and Mrs. FSBO. Viewed from our side of the fence, we fully realize all the valuable tools we have in the form of expertise, broker cooperation, multiple listing service, etc., to get a property sold and it may seem incredible to us that owners would want to deprive themselves of these advantages and expect to sell their own homes without hiring a real estate professional. If you were to take the time to conduct your own survey among the FSBO families in your town, you would be able to compile a list of their reasons which would resemble this one.

---

1. In the past, their transactions with one or more real estate agents have been unsatisfactory. There was the agent who:

   "took the listing and we never heard from him again until he called to ask us to extend it";

   "never advertised it in the paper and only held one Open House";

   "kept wanting us to reduce the house even though we listed at the price he told us he could get for it";

   "brought us a low offer and got very annoyed when we wouldn't accept--said we might not get another one";

   "We just didn't get along with the agent. We wanted to cancel the listing but we couldn't get the broker to let us and, when it finally ran out, it was winter so it was too late";

   and more horror stories.

2. They feel that an agent would not do anything they cannot do for themselves to sell the home so they might as well save the commission which, in any case, they regard as too much for the little work it takes to do the job.

3. The family wants to be "in control" of who has access to their home and when. They do not want agents interrupting them at any time for showings or, even worse, have them using a lockbox and walking in without warning.

4. The owners enjoy the challenge of finding a buyer. They do not necessarily consider an agent overpaid, but figure they can put the commission saved towards the

downpayment on their next house.

5. There is no strong motivation to sell. If a buyer comes along who will pay the price asked, they will make a good profit and buy a nicer home; if not, they are content to continue living in the property.

In analyzing these reasons, you can readily conclude that you must find out which of them applies to the FSBO you are currently hoping to convert. Your efforts are more likely to bring results when applied to the first three categories.

Consider, too, the reception a real estate listing agent can expect from homeowners who have bravely made the decision to sell their own home; it is likely to range from icy politeness to abruptness and even what you will regard as rudeness. You will be less inclined to be frightened away by this attitude when you understand that it is the FSBO defense against attack. Just as a real estate agent is sometimes hampered by fear of rejection, Mr./Mrs. FSBO have their own particular worry with which to contend. They know they are the fox being chased by a relentless field of real estate agents in a special type of listing hunt. They fear being run into a corner so that, in one vulnerable moment, they would find themselves saying "yes" to an aggressive agent instead of being able to hold the field at bay and continuing to tell each one "no". Sometimes the FSBO's who resist the hardest initially are the ones who give up the soonest and are actually the easiest ones to list.

Once you appreciate the philosophy of Mr. and Mrs. FSBO, you realize that it is going to take a special technique to persuade them to allow you to list their home. Scare tactics, saying how hard and tedious it is for an owner to sell a home these days and unpleasant aggressiveness will win you no FSBO friends or listings. Successful agents with pleasing personalities list FSBO homes through patient perseverance, gentle persuasion, tact, understanding and a sincere wish to help them solve their real estate problems.

Organizing Your FSBO Campaign

The best sources for leads to homes for sale by owner are:

1. Advertisements from the classified columns in local newspapers;

2. FSBO magazines;

3.   FSBO yard signs;

4.   FSBO cards on bulletin boards;

5.   Referrals.

In Figure 7 you will find a useful form for record-keeping which, as in any other type of prospecting, is essential. Photocopy a supply and file the pages in a three-ring binder. Insert another page in front of these which you have divided into columns headed with the various three-digit prefixes used by the local telephone system.

Clip the FSBO ads from the newspaper every day and from magazines the same day issued. Most of them will contain only a telephone number as a lead to the homeowner; use it for identification purposes. Write the number in the appropriate column of your binder's front page; as you clip new ads (or bring in leads from other sources) you can quickly see if the new ads are for a home which already has a record-page or if you have a new prospect.

Tape the first ad you clip for each home in the space provided on the form; when future ads contain more information, these can be taped to the back of the page. Note under "Source" the date of the ad. File these pages in numerical order by phone number; later, once you know the addresses, you can set up a cross-reference system so that you can locate the appropriate record-page by knowing either a phone number or address. Do this by adding a section to the binder to contain, in alphabetical order, a page for each street in the area you are covering; an alternative is a page for the letter of the alphabet when the number of streets starting with a particular one are few. On these pages, write the address in the left column and show the phone number in the righthand one which will enable you to turn to the appropriate record-page for the property.

Discover The FSBO's Address

Your chances of listing a house you have never seen are slim indeed but you'll never get your foot inside the front door if you have no idea where it is located. Most FSBO ads will omit the address so now is the time to put on your Sherlock Holmes disguise and logically discover what that is.

Cross-reference books in which you can look up the telephone number to determine the address and ownership of a property include the city directory, telephone company's

Condo ___ ; House ____   PHONE: _____

SOURCE
                    Date: Owner _____
FSBO sign   _____   Address _____
Bulletin card   _____   _____
Referral by   _____   *Listing date* _____ *Result of* _____
Advertisement   _____

                                         ┌──────────────────────────────┐
                                         │   *CONTACTS WITH SELLERS*   │
                                         Letter
┌─────────────────────────────┐   Date   Comment
│   │   _____
│ *(Affix copy of advertisement here)* │ _____
│   │   _____
└─────────────────────────────┘   _____

Followup ads noticed: (weekly)
    Media   Date   Phone
_____   _____   Date
_____   _____
_____   _____
_____   _____
_____   _____
_____   _____

FSBO LISTED BY OTHER BROKER: Visit to owner
Co   Appx. date
Price   Agt   Date/Reaction: _____
Co   Appx   date   _____
Price   Agt   _____

RESULT   Other:

Figure 7. For Sale By Owner record sheet. This page can be enlarged
to 170% on a photocopy machine to fit handily on 8.5" x 11" paper and
provide work forms to for a 3-ring binder.

cross-reference guide and "Cole's Directory"; at least one of these should be available at the reference department of your local library. When you begin FSBO farming, read through real estate classified advertising in back issues of Sunday newspapers to learn how long the seller has been trying to find a buyer for the home; once you are reading classifieds on a regular basis, you will pick up each new FSBO as they start advertising. The back issues can be found either at the library or at the publisher's office.

If you are unable to trace an address from the cross-reference guides, the last resort is to call the number in the ad and ask for it so that you can drive by. A real estate professional is a person who is well-informed but, as you are only now educating yourself about this particular property, you do not want to identify yourself as a real estate agent to the person who answers the telephone. You may prefer to ask someone to make the call for you.

Once you know the address of a FSBO home, regardless of the source of the lead, drive by it slowly several times. Note its style, condition, curb appeal, how it compares with other homes for sale in the area and the type of sign the owner has put in the front yard. If the sign is one made by a professional signmaker, it is an indication that this owner will not lightly change his decision to market his own property.

Follow the same procedure with homes advertised on cards on bulletin boards. Drive by homes which are brought to your attention by referors and note the same information for these and the ones you notice yourself as you drive around town. Instead of following the shortest route to the office, grocery store, club meeting, etc., take the extra time to reach your destination via a variety of routes and look for FSBO signs.

After driving by a prospective FSBO listing, although you have not yet seen the interior, you can now do some research in current and past issues of the multilist books to get a preliminary idea of a price range for it so you can judge how realistic the seller is being with the asking price (if it was advertised).

Contacting The Owner

You cannot list a house before you get inside the door so this is your first objective. The average agent makes no more than one contact per FSBO, leaves a business card and hopes for the best but striving for the FSBO listing definitely takes more than that.

An effective FSBO contact program is comprised of a steady stream of letters, visits and phone calls. Don't give up until the house is listed (by you or a competitor) or it is sold by the owner. Even if the owners apparently change their mind and remove their home from the market, add them to your SOI farm; they thought about selling seriously enough to try it themselves so, next time, you want to get the listing before the FSBO sign goes up in their yard!

Send A Letter First

Many real estate agents hate writing letters and knocking on a FSBO door doesn't hold much appeal for them either. It is much easier to pick up the phone even though one must surely know that Mr. and Mrs. FSBO are very tired of answering it hoping it is a prospect calling but hearing instead the voice of yet another faceless agent wanting to list their home. Small wonder, then, that the agent gets a negative reaction to the unwelcome interruption.

Begin your campaign with a good letter; compose your own or use the sample shown in Figure 8. It is advisable to type this for each FSBO you are contacting but, if time will not permit and you do not have word processing equipment, get a supply of the body of this letter printed on company letterhead. You can then handwrite the date and an appropriate salutation on each letter and sign your name. For better impact, add a postscript which is personalized for the recipients, i.e. "Your home looked so inviting from the road when I drove by today. I'd love to see the inside!"

Each letter should be mailed with enclosures. Your business card is an obvious one but include, too, a useful handout imprinted with your identification. This could be tips on showing a home at its best; list of names, addresses and phone numbers of lenders or escrow companies or schools or recreational centers; a card on which you have worked out the monthly principal and interest payment a buyer would have to make based on their asking price on a typical mortgage currently available locally; etc. The better the enclosure(s), the greater your chance will be of the recipients keeping it for reference. When they do, they are reminded about you by seeing your name and affiliation again. This mail approach allows your photograph to be seen by the sellers on the letterhead and/or business card and gives them a friendly face to associate with your name and, later, your voice.

Home & Hearth Realty

12 State Street
Keston, CA 00000
Ph. (000) 000-0000

Jan Carpenter
Sales Associate
Home: (000) 000-0000

August 12, 1991

Dear Mr. and Mrs. (name):

Your house for sale advertisement in the "Keston Times" caught my eye and I would like to offer my good wishes for your success.

May I come by and see your home? I respect your desire to sell it yourself and my request is NOT made so that I can try to convince you to list with me! It is my job to match the right buyer with the right home so I need to be familiar with every home that is currently offered for sale, not just those with brokers' signs in the front yards. To me, your "For Sale By Owner" property is just as important as those and it would be very helpful to me to be permitted to view its interior.

If you've never previously tried to market a house yourself, here are some tips which you may find useful:

Is Your Property Ready for Viewing?

Toys, boxes and other objects removed from entry, halls, stairs? Front entrance spic, span and welcoming? Screens/storm windows fastened? A bright light bulb in every fixture? Appliances, faucets, etc. in good working order? Kitchen neat with countertops cleared? Closets organized and uncluttered? Pets secured?

When Buyers Want To Know, Can You Answer These Questions?

Square footage of home and room measurements? Lot size? Locations of public and private schools, churches, shops, bus stop, shops, recreational facilities? Cost of utilities for the past year?

In the event that there is anything I can do as a courtesy to assist you with the sale of your home, please call me any time. It is very possible that you will have questions or need some real estate forms as you progress and I would certainly be glad to help in any way that I can.

Meanwhile, I would very much appreciate the opportunity to look through your home and look forward to hearing from you soon.

Best wishes for your success,

Jan Carpenter

Figure 8. Letter to homeowners who are trying the FSBO method.

Make A Telephone Call

Follow up your first letter with a telephone call the day after you anticipate your letter will have arrived. You have done your homework and are now ready to identify yourself as a real estate professional to the person who answers the phone. Mr. or Mrs. FSBO will be on guard against a pitch for a listing once the voice of an agent is heard so avoid any hint of that topic.

You might say, "This is Jan Carpenter. I sent you a letter a few days ago with some information which I thought might be useful to you while you're trying to sell your home. Did you receive it yet?"

If there is some hesitation in response as Mr. or Mrs. FSBO tries to recall who Jan Carpenter is and what the letter was about, add, "I'm with Home & Hearth Realty and I sent you a little card on which I had worked out what the monthly payments might be for the person who buys your lovely home. I hope it did arrive okay."

Go on to ask if the person has heard that ... ... (give another tidbit of current information such as a special interest rate being offered by a particular lender or a change in VA or FHA rates).

To finish your call, inquire if they had a good number of people at their Open House the previous weekend. Mention that you would very much enjoy seeing their home but did not want to interrupt them during their Open House. Would it be convenient if you stopped by this afternoon or would sometime tomorrow be better?

Be prepared when you phone or visit to be told that the FSBO's intend to sell themselves. Don't be discouraged, you already know this. Assure them that you respect their intentions and are not calling to solicit a listing. Explain that you like to keep yourself informed of everything that is presently for sale and that's the only reason you are asking to see their home.

Another FSBO line of defense is that they have a friend or relative in real estate so, if they were not doing their own selling, that person would get the listing. Again, don't be put off. They may or may not have such a connection but press on with your program. The other agent might be a firm believer in grandmother's advice not to work for a close friend or relative if the harmony is to happily continue and would just as soon not be asked to take such a listing. Or that other agent may be staying away from the scene deliberately offering no help or advice at all figuring that the sooner the FSBO flounders, the faster the listing will fall into his lap. As you continue your campaign, his attitude will contrast unfavorably with your friendliness, interest and continuing willingness to be of service and could easily win you the listing.

It's Now Time To Meet Face-To-Face

We must always remember that we cannot hope to list the home until we can get inside it. The next step is a face-to-face meeting. If your telephone call did not result in an appointment, simply drop by the house to give Mr. and Mrs. FSBO another useful handout. You can say, "I was just driving by and thought I'd stop for a minute and see if you were home. I have this pamphlet for you which shows the fees charged by the various escrow companies around town."

Develop the conversation by inquiring how the marketing is going and does the homeowner have any questions you may be able to answer. If you don't know an answer, explain that you will find out which gives you another reason to return. If the owner seems receptive to your visit, ask if you might take a quick look through the home. Otherwise, say that you would appreciate a chance to see inside and can return next afternoon, or would this evening be more convenient?

Whether you get inside the home due to your telephone call or the "drop-by" visit, do not verbally attempt to list the house the first time. If you do, you seriously risk forfeiting any rapport you have built to this point. Instead, show the host/hostess the courtesy they would expect from an invited guest. Express your interest in what you see with compliments on the home's various features and/or decor. Silently observe the house as you would be doing if you there to list it so that you can later work up a good CMA (see chapter 8).

While touring the home, or before if the opportunity presents itself, ask the reason for the impending move. The response, if a true one is given, will indicate motivation or lack of same. Concentrate your FSBO prospecting on those who have a positive motivation to sell. The day after you have toured a FSBO home, remember to send a handwritten thank you note.

One-Party Listing

Never lie to Mr. and Mrs. FSBO. Don't try to get a listing

by pretending to have a buyer for their home. Believe me, they've heard that line before. If you honestly do have a party whom you feel would be a prospect for the home, ask if you can have a "one-party listing". Explain that, by agreeing to this, they would commit to pay your office an agreed-upon commission in the event that the named party did make an offer-to-purchase and they accepted it. Assure them that such a listing does not interrupt their own efforts to find a buyer, it simply adds another dimension to their marketing program and yours is confined to just the one prospect at this time.

It is my opinion that it is better to ask for a one-party listing when you have a prospect for a FSBO home than to ask up front the blanket question, "If I should find a buyer for your home, would you be willing to pay a commission to my office?" Unless you are dealing with very knowledgeable sellers, their agreement to such an arrangement tends to give them the illusion that you will actively market their home and seek a buyer for them. We know this is not true; such an informal arrangement does not merit serious marketing effort by an agent, nor is there the benefit of multiple listing. Yet, when they are ultimately ready to seek professional help, you may find that you are not even considered to act as their official listing agent because you've already had your chance and failed to produce results.

Be Of Genuine Help

Each contact you make with Mr. and Mrs. FSBO serves to establish you in their minds as a friendly real estate professional who seems interested in their problems and genuinely wants to be helpful. Whenever you spot a newspaper clipping, or have any other printed item, that could in any way tie in with their marketing efforts, drop it in the mail with your card and a short note.

The signs used by FSBO's are usually homemade; offer to lend professional open house signs to them for use over the weekend. This affords you with a reason to see the sellers on Friday and again on Monday when you collect the signs. Repeat the offer each weekend. Provide them with blank deposit receipts (offer to purchase forms) with your compliments.

Always be as helpful as you can to Mr. and Mrs. FSBO. The service you provide will be welcomed once they find you are not one of those aggressive listors but are a friendly, helpful person. You will increase your chance of getting the listing when the FSBO family is weary of the demands of do-it-yourself marketing. In the event they happen to get a buyer, you may still benefit by selling them a replacement home and perhaps even list the home that the buyers must sell before they can close on the FSBO home.

Pre- & Post-Weekend Contact Essential

It is important to have a reason to touch bases with FSBO's on Thursdays or Fridays and again on Monday or Tuesday. Prior to the weekend, if you are not lending signs, you can say you noticed their ad in the paper for the open house they are going to do on Sunday and phoned to wish them luck. If there was no ad, go by their house to see them and say that you missed seeing it this week. A missed ad can mean that Mr. and Mrs. FSBO have had enough of trying to sell the house themselves and are ready to consider professional help.

Following their weekend's Open House, stop by on Monday to show your interest in their progress. As each weekend comes and goes without a sale, the likelihood of finding them ready to turn the job over to you on any Monday increases. Always leave a handout with your business card attached when you call on them.

Through the program outlined here, the owners of the various FSBO homes are gradually getting to know and trust you and sample your expertise. In turn, you are learning about them and their real estate objectives. You will be able to judge when the time is right to approach them for the listing.

FSBO On The Job

As real estate professionals, a new listing represents to us a potential period of at least three months of sustained selling effort. What do Mr. and Mrs. FSBO anticipate when they "list" with themselves? Usually they expect their task will be fairly simple and that a buyer will appear in two or three weeks. Let's look at a typical FSBO scenario to gain some perception of the situation we may be tackling when we try to list a FSBO property.

The decision to sell by the FSBO method has been made, hopes and enthusiasm are high. Mrs. FSBO straightens up the house while Mr. FSBO makes up a yard sign, inserts an ad in the paper and buys a blank sales contract from the local office supply store. While they wait for potential buyers to come through the door, they even flip through the pages of a "how to sell your own home" book and think how easy it's going to be.

By the end of the first weekend, a few curious people and some of the neighbors have come in to look. We generally call them "lookie lou's" but to Mr. and Mrs. FSBO they are "prospects". Of course, they have been outnumbered by the real estate agents who have stopped by, several of whom have said they have a buyer for the house. It seems to the sellers that they have a hot property and it will only be a short time before the house is sold. It could even sell to one of the "buyers" those agents said they had because they will come by on their own when they read the ad in the newspaper classifieds.

Another weekend passes and a few more people have visited as a result of the yard sign and newspaper ad. Nobody has made an offer to purchase but Mr. and Mrs. FSBO feel they are getting a lot more activity than they had last summer when it was listed with that agent who did nothing so they are not discouraged. It was easy for them to turn down the new batch of real estate agents who phoned and dropped in over the weekend wanting to list the house. As Mrs. FSBO said, "There are so many of them, it's a good thing that we seldom hear from any agent more than once!"

By the end of the third weekend, staying home to answer the phone and hold Open House is getting rather tedious. It would have been so much more enjoyable to have spent Saturday fishing at the lake and then attended the football game on Sunday afternoon. Maybe next weekend they ought to have a break from this? No, better not, they might miss Mr. and Mrs. Buyer.

After the fourth weekend, Mr. and Mrs. FSBO are pretty discouraged. To begin with, they were busy with everyday living demands during the week and forgot until it was too late to renew their newspaper ad. As a result, only two couples came by off the yard sign. One couple was really rude about the decor, Mrs. FSBO's personal choice, and said they would have to spend a lot of money fixing the place up. Mr. FSBO was trying to watch the golf match on television and the second couple distracted him with their questions so much he completely missed the action on the 18th hole. Both are tired of their FSBO roles and now is the right time for you, the one persistent, helpful, pleasing real estate professional who has been with them all the way so far, to step in and solve their problem. By that time, you will have read Chapters 9 and 10 of this book and be ready to write up the listing!

8

Exploring The
Expireds

A final source for listings is homes which have previously been on the market for sale but had not sold at the time the listing periods ended. These homes are found in the following categories:

1.   Homes on which you were the listing agent;

2.   Homes listed with your office but with another agent;

3.   Homes listed with other brokers' offices;

4.   FSBC properties.

The listings may have just expired or could have ended weeks, or even months, ago. Before we explore these possibilities, however, we should first consider listings which you presently have upon which the expiration date is imminent.

Renewing Prior To Expiration

At the time you took the listing, you and the owners agreed upon a certain marketing period. The expiration date of any listing you take should be entered into your daytimer together with a notation two weeks in advance to alert you to take action.

Since you are a conscientious agent and have tried diligently to get the house sold, it is possible that it remains on the market without an accepted offer to purchase two weeks prior to listing expiration date due to one or more of the following common reasons:

1. Sellers will not lower listed price, even though it is too high, and will not negotiate seriously on offers;

2. Adverse market conditions, i.e. high interest rates;

3. Bad time of year for home sales;

4. Sellers (or tenants) do not always cooperate with showings;

5. Property does not show well due to poor housekeeping, an unfriendly dog is present during showings, or failure of sellers to get needed maintenance done.

If the reason is one of the first three, even though you may have failed to get a price reduction earlier, make a final attempt. Set up an appointment to meet with the sellers and take along an up-to-date CMA (competitive market analysis--see Chapter 9) to illustrate the need for a lower price. Go over with them once again the marketing you have done in the past weeks to find a buyer for the home which, so far, has not produced one willing to pay the listed price. Explain to the owners why you feel a price reduction would regenerate excitement about the home among fellow real estate agents and their buyers. Tell them about special marketing efforts you will make to attract a buyer for their repriced home.

Have a listing status change form ready in your briefcase to complete for the new price. As you are filling it out, comment that you are very pleased about the new price and you would like some time for your marketing work to take effect. Remind them that the listing is due to run out in two weeks and suggest that they extend it now.

If you acquired the listing in off-season and, now that it is about to expire, a better time of year is approaching, go to the sellers and review your marketing efforts with them again. Show them sales statistics in the area for the period and explain that there are not many buyers at this time of year but, you expect activity to pick up in the next four months just as it did at the same time last year. Back up your statement with sales statistics for similar periods of the previous year. Ask for an extension.

In the event the reason the home has not sold falls into either of the last two categories, or if there is a pricing problem which the sellers adamantly refuse to adjust, you should ask yourself whether or not you want this listing to be renewed. A listing is a responsibility and an expense; if it is one that is virtually impossible to sell regardless of how hard you try to interest a buyer, this broker would not seek an extension.

There are occasions, too, when you will have found your relationship with the sellers to be completely at odds. Perhaps you feel obligated to try for a listing renewal but your heart is not in it and you secretly hope the sellers will turn you down. When you are confronted with a listing such as this, before you approach the sellers for a renewal consult your office broker. It is possible that another agent may be able to work better with these particular sellers and, if the house sells, you would receive a consideration.

Renewing Your Own Listings After Expiration

There are times when one of your listings will not be renewed simply because the sellers want to take it off the market. They have no complaint at all with your work but have either changed their minds about selling or feel they want to wait until another time.

That, of course, is their prerogative but don't wait for them to call you. Keep in regular touch. Send little notecards, phone or stop by at least once each month to inform them of market activity in their area, interest rates, etc. If you neglect them, between now and the time they think about putting the home on the market again, they may have been wooed and won by another real estate agent.

Newly Expired Listings

There will be a standard procedure followed at your office to keep you aware of in-house expirations and you can learn which listings of other brokers have just gone off the market through your local multilist service.

One must be exceedingly careful when pursuing newly expireds especially if the listing is held by another office. Approaching, without due verification, a homeseller as soon as you read a report that the listing has expired can lead to serious misunderstandings and even charges of ethics violation.

While the multilist computer will automatically report expirations immediately they occur, it is very possible that the listing agent already has a signed renewal in hand but has not yet got it into the multilist system. Another problem occurs when a sale on a listed property is either contingent or pending; the computer indicates the listing has expired when the last day of its term has passed unless the agent has submitted a renewal in a timely manner.

Test the accuracy of the reported expiration by first referring to multilist reports of contingent and pending sales. If you find a report for the "expired" property, telephone the listing agent and ask about its current status. If you do not find such a report, contact the listor and ask, "Do you have a signed renewal on your listing at (address)?" When the response you receive concerning status indicates that the listing is still active, or if the agent tells you that a renewal has already been signed, eliminate this one from your prospects. Otherwise you are at liberty to try to acquire the listing.

When properties are listed by other agents in your office, it does not make for a good working relationship to charge out and try to list them as soon as the expiration date comes around. Be courteous. Ask the agent if he/she is trying to get the renewal; if the reply is negative, the road is open for you.

Your chances of signing a newly expired listing depend on the sellers' opinion of events during the time it was on the market. Obviously, they have a reason for not renewing and you must find out what it is. The cause will probably be among the following:

1. The agent is not keeping proper track of the listing and has forgotten to ask for the renewal in a timely manner;

2. The seller, while not unhappy with the efforts of the agent, wants to consider listing with another office in the hope that:

    (a) A different marketing approach would be more successful;

    (b) A larger office might produce more potential buyers (or) smaller office would give the listing more personal attention;

3. The seller is not satisfied with the agent's efforts and intends to choose another agent to represent the home;

4. Market conditions, or time of year, have made the seller decide to postpone listing it again;

5. Circumstances have changed and the seller no longer wants to move.

Contacting The Seller

Time is of the essence in securing an expired listing. A number of agents will be competing for it and you need to act quickly. A personal visit is the preferred action to take but, when you ring the sellers' doorbell to ask for an appointment, you should be well prepared to do an on-the-spot presentation if necessary.

Research the property. When was it acquired by the present owner? Look through multilist records for at least the past year to find out when it was first put on the market for sale. Note which agents have had the listing, the different listed prices and terms offered. Check comparable sales in the area during its marketing periods to gauge whether the price asked for the subject home was in line with those that sold. If multilist photo brochures are available for the home, assess as best you can from those the curb appeal of the home. These facts will give you an overview of the situation, an idea of how motivated the seller is and whether the listing has been properly priced. Work up a current CMA as described in Chapter 9.

When the seller opens the front door, introduce yourself and hand him a business card. Your conversation might proceed something like this:

You: I noticed that your home is no longer listed and was wondering if you have changed your mind about moving?

Seller: No, not really. It just seems that we're not making any progress and I think it must be because it's the wrong time of year (or financing is hard to get). I thought I might wait a few months before I put the house back on the market.

You: You're right about this being a difficult time. However, buyers are still out there. Our sales reports show us that homes, especially ones as nice as yours, are continuing to sell even if the pace is a bit slower than we'd all like. It's simply a bigger challenge to us now to work harder and find the qualified buyer who is right for the homes we represent. What is your name, by the way?

Seller: Jack Friscoe.

You: Mr. Friscoe, I can understand that you're feeling discouraged about the prospects for selling your home any time soon, but I really don't think you should be.

****I did some research into the potential market for a home such as yours and I came up with some interesting ideas that I would like to go over with you. Do you have some time now, or would tomorrow be better?

It is possible that your opening comment regarding the house no longer being listed will surprise the seller and the dialog will differ. He will tell you that he has it listed with Such-And-Such Company. Explain that you know they have had the listing for the past ninety days but you thought it had expired. Ask if he has already signed a renewal of the listing extending it for a longer period. If he tells you that he has done so, apologize for disturbing him and leave promptly. It is more likely, since you verified the expiration before calling at the home, that the seller will say he did not know the listing expired. The thought will probably cross his mind that the agent forgot to bring this to his attention which contrasts with your alertness and he will be receptive to what you have to say.

Explain that since his home has been reported as an expired listing in the multilist system that this means any marketing efforts by cooperating brokers are presently at a standstill. Tell him that you really like his home and would appreciate a chance to get some exciting things rolling for him. Say that you have been doing some research (see comment preceded by ** in the preceding dialog and continue from there).

If it turns out that this seller was unhappy with the previous agent and was almost counting the days to expiration, you may find yourself listening to a recital of all that the agent could have done and didn't and those things that were done which met with the seller's disapproval. Do not encourage these remarks. Listen politely and try to change the subject as tactfully as you can. Tell him that you can understand he is feeling somewhat discouraged right now but wouldn't this be a good time to put the past behind him and look to the future? Go on with the dialog starting from **. You will find more ideas to help you acquire the listing in Chapter 10.

Past Expired Listings

Review the listings which your office and other brokers'

offices have held in the past but which expired unsold. Note the date on which a listing was lost and go through multilist computer references since then (or go through back issues of the catalog) to see if the home ever came back on the market. If it did and sold, delete that one as a possibility.

Make a record card for each home that remains in the same ownership and add it to your listing prospect file. Jot down on the card any data concerning its subsequent relisting if you did find any. Attach a brochure (or photocopy) clipped from the multilist book. Check market activity in the neighborhood since the expiration date and add to your card.

There is no panic in pursuing past expireds as not too many agents bother to work these once they've been off the market for more than a month. Yours can be a leisurely courtship. Begin with a brief letter to the owners (a sample is shown in Figure 9). Follow it up with a telephone call to try to discover if the owners still have any interest in selling the home:

You: Mrs. Homeowner, this is Jan Carpenter at Home & Hearth Realty. Did you receive the letter I sent you a few days ago?

Mrs. H.: Yes.

You: May I ask what caused you and Mr. H. to change your minds about selling your home last (September)?

Mrs. H.: Well, we just got tired of the whole thing. We'd had it for sale for several months and we never knew when we got up in the morning if somebody was going to phone during the day and want to come right over. I felt I had to keep everything looking nice and that really got old. We had wanted to buy a new condominium because this house is actually more space than we need now but it didn't seem as if we'd get a buyer so we decided to give up the idea of moving and stay here.

You: I can understand how you must have felt at that time, Mrs. H. In the past few months, market conditions have improved and prospective buyers are a lot more serious now. We've had some good sales recently of homes similar to yours. I would very much like to meet you and see the inside of your home. Would it be okay if I come by later today or sometime tomorrow? What time is best for you?

Mrs. H.: Oh, I don't think there would be any point in

Home & Hearth Realty

12 State Street
Keston, CA 00000
Ph. (000) 000-0000

Jan Carpenter
Sales Associate
Home: (000) 000-0000

May 10, 1992

Dear Mr. and Mrs. (name):

Last summer, your very attractive home was offered for sale but it has not appeared in the Keston multilist catalog since October. It occurred to me that you may not be aware of the exciting happenings in today's real estate market.

Already this year, home sales have increased 19.7% over the same period a year ago. There is a flurry of activity as buyers hurry to take advantage of the lower mortgage interest rates currently available. We are extremely optimistic that the pace will continue during the next few months.

I showed your home once last year when you had it listed with another broker's office. It impressed me then and I feel that it has very special appeal for the right buyers. Are you still interested in selling?

Home & Hearth Realty has been established in Keston since 1977 and, over the past 15 years, has gained a fine reputation for service to the community. The twenty full-time real estate professionals in our State Street office comprise an enthusiastic, hard-working team which has succeeded in getting the job done for countless satisfied sellers.

Would you like to know the price range in which you could expect your home to sell this year? It would be my pleasure to prepare a complimentary analysis for you and I would appreciate an opportunity to discuss with you my ideas for an effective marketing program which I am confident would bring the desired result. In the next few days, I will telephone you to arrange a convenient time for me to stop by your home.

Sincerely,

Jan Carpenter

Figure 9. Letter to owners of homes with past expired listings.

having you do that. We've decided now to stay where we are.

You: Yes, I understand you've given up the idea of moving but I would still like to see your home and I think you and Mr. H. would be interested to hear what's currently happening. I don't want to take up a lot of your time so why don't I just bring some information by for you to look over at your leisure and perhaps you will be kind enough to give me a quick tour of your home. When would be a convenient time? How about 7 o'clock this evening or would tomorrow afternoon at 3 be better for you?

If Mrs. Homeowner continues to resist your request for an appointment, end your conversation on a friendly note by saying that you will keep in touch. Send her a notecard thanking her for the information she gave you.

Start contacting this prospect on a regular basis with tidbits of information about sales activity in the neighborhood. Use notecards and the telephone for this purpose. Each time, ask politely for an appointment to see the home. Take time to build a friendly rapport with these homeowners and then drop by to meet them with a handout one day when you are in the area. By now you will have learned what type of housing they intended to get if their home had sold so your handout could be a brochure on a particularly nice property which fits the description.

You: Mrs. H, I'm Jan Carpenter from Home & Hearth Realty. I was in the neighborhood and I wanted to drop off this brochure for you. It's a condo which just came on the market and, when I saw it, I thought about you. It seems to have everything that you told me you wanted if you had sold your home last (September).

Mrs. H.: Oh, that does look nice.

You: I know you've told me you're not going to sell now so you won't be buying either. Even so, wouldn't it be kind of fun to take a look at this new listing? If you're not busy, we could drive over there now and see it. Or would this evening be better?

This technique has a good chance of resulting in a showing for you. When you take her through it, whether or not she wants to buy it, her interest in moving will probably be revived. Even if she declines to go to see the condo, this evidence of your continuing interest in her will probably earn you an invitation to see the inside of her present home. You are making progress a step at a time.

FSBO Expirations

There is no multilist system to alert you to FSBO expireds so you have to search for them yourself. From the FSBO records you have compiled and contacting methods described in Chapter 7, you will know when those owners currently trying to sell their own homes have either succeeeded or given up.

To widen this prospecting field, spend some time going through the classifieds in the Sunday issues of past newspapers prior to the time you became a FSBO farmer. Decide whether to research the past six months, nine months or one year and then start your research with the first issue for that period. It is easier to catch the first time a FSBO advertised (i.e. the beginning of a "FSBO listing period") when you read the classifieds in chronological order as issued than it is if you work back from present to past. Jot down the following information for each property on 3"x5" cards:

```
OWNER                          PHONE

HOUSE/CONDO ADDRESS

FIRST AD DATE

OTHER AD DATES

PRICE--$

PRICE ADJUSTMENTS/DATES

OTHER DATA
```

Usually newspaper ads do not contain owner's name or the address but if your local paper separates houses from condos in its columns, you can draw a line through the non-applicable word. Under "Other data", jot down facts provided on rooms, amenities, neighborhood, financing, etc. The date of the final advertisement you see for a particular property is usually a good indication of the last week the owner attempted to find a buyer.

After your reading is done, separate the cards without addresses from the others and look the telephone numbers up in a cross reference directory compiled by the telephone company or other publisher. Once you have addresses on the cards, take each one in turn and refer to the multilist service to see whether the FSBO property was listed by a professional agent. If it was but did not sell, clip the brochure (or photocopy it if you are working with a reference copy of a multilist book) and attach it to the card. You may find some properties that were listed more than once; note the details. On sold properties, file their cards for future reference or dispose of them.

There will be some properties which do not appear in multilist indicating either that the owners never listed with a professional and still own the property, or that they did effect a private sale. The only way to determine which is correct without phoning the owner is to check county records of ownership.

Once your research is finished, you will have a number of homes and condos which their owners at one time wanted to sell but, to this day, remain unsold. Proceed to contact them adapting the methods described earlier and in Chapter 7.

Your Best Service

When you succeed in listing an expired, you are faced with a double challenge. Not only do you want to do a good job and get the property sold but you must give this listing special attention. Your seller may be skeptical about the chances of your finding a buyer; he has either been disillusioned about the effectiveness of real estate agents by past experience, or is one who may still secretly believe the owner of a home is its best salesperson.

Be sure to list the home at the proper market price as indicated by a carefully-researched CMA; you don't want to have to ask for a price reduction from such sellers early in the listing term! Touch bases with the sellers weekly; tell them about any activity regarding the house including buyers' and other agents' reactions and the progress of your marketing program.

Follow the suggestions outlined in Chapter 11; use your ingenuity and do everything possible to secure a buyer. When you represent the owners of expired listings, you have a fine opportunity to prove to them that a true real estate professional will solve their problems and get the job done.

9

Listing   Preparation

$\mathcal{B}$e confident that sooner or later your farming work, if properly done, will bring results so be ready to handle your first listing appointment. It will go smoothly if you are well prepared with the necessary materials and information and have the right attitude.

Presentation Book

An attractive presentation book is a real asset during a listing interview and you should make one for yourself now. Purchase a distinctive 3-ring binder (8.5" x 11" size), colored mounting paper, a supply of transparent sheet covers and tabbed section dividers. The binder is better than a scrapbook because you can easily add new items to the appropriate sections and can update material as necessary.

The following is a suggested list of contents for your book. You will already be able to assemble quite a number of these items and can add more as you acquire them.

1.   Certificates of achievement:

Pre-licensing courses;

Continuing real estate education;

Seminar and convention attendance;

        G.R.I. and/or other designations;

        Company awards;

        Community service.

2. Membership certificates in National Association of REALTORS, etc.

3. Copy of real estate license.

4. Photograph of yourself and brief biography.

5. Photograph of your office.

6. Company brochures.

7. Newspaper clippings about yourself and the Company.

8. List of properties you have listed and/or sold.

9. List of properties listed and/or sold by your office.

10. Letters of appreciation from clients and customers.

11. Newspaper clippings concerning the neighborhood. Clip suitable items as you spot them, mount on sheets in protectors by area and insert those appropriate to the presentation in the book prior to leaving for the listing appointment.

12. Reasons for listing a home versus for sale by owner.

13. Planned marketing campaign:

        Photograph of your Company "For Sale" sign;

        Clippings of newspaper and/or magazine classified and display advertisements placed by your Company;

        Samples of direct mail to neighbors, etc.;

        Samples of flyers sent to cooperating brokers;

        Clipping from the multilist catalog showing typical brochure;

        Tips for seller on how to prepare home for showing at its best;

Home warranty insurance programs;

Financial sheet showing current interest rates and loan types available.

14. Example of sales contract form.

15. Example of an exclusive right to sell listing agreement & disclosure forms

Divide the pages into sections separated by titled dividers and mount each section's material on a different shade of paper. The book can be used as a visual aid to accompany your spoken words so arrange the sections to suit your proposed dialog. If you are seated around a table in kitchen or diningroom with the book open in front of the sellers, you can turn the pages as you speak and it will help you to remember your "lines". This will lessen the chance of you overlooking important points and will give you confidence. Even if you are a new agent, your presentation book can be impressive both in size and quality of content.

Listing Appointment Preliminaries

When you are invited to the home of an owner who wants to sell, your first impulse may be to jump into your car and drive right over with presentation book in hand. Not so fast, please! First you need to prepare a "competitive" market analysis (sometimes called "comparative" or CMA) which could take several hours, longer if much research is indicated. Allow time to do this when making your appointment with the owner.

There are two questions that every homeowner is going to ask you during your listing appointment, "How much can you get for my home? How quickly can you get it sold?" These questions are so important to a seller that you must be able to give an intelligent response. A wild guess certainly won't do and this is one time when a reply of "I don't know, but I'll get the information" won't help you secure the listing. While you're back at the office doing the CMA that you should have had with you in the first place, another better-prepared agent will be getting the seller's signature on the listing agreement.

If you are contacted by the owner of a house with which you are not at all familiar, ask a few questions at the time the appointment is made to determine basic information:

1. Address of property;

2. Style of home (ranch, tri-level, etc.);

3. Number of bedrooms, baths;

4. Does it have familyroom, diningroom, garage;

5. Age of the home;

6. Owners of record as shown on the deed;

7. How long the sellers have owned the home;

8. Reason for selling.

If your prospective listing has resulted from farming, calling on owners who are trying to sell themselves, or is a home with which you are familiar for other reasons, you will already know the answers to most of those questions. When the contact comes from "out of the blue", drive by the property right away to familiarize yourself with its style and appearance as well as the neighborhood.

Legally, the signatures of every owner of record must appear on the listing agreement for a property in order for a sale to be valid. If you intend to list a home, you must determine its exact ownership (how title is held). Records at the county recorder's office are one source for this information; asking the owner to show you a copy of the deed is another. The best way to acquire it, however, is to order an Owners & Encumbrances Report (commonly referred to as an O&E) from a title company; it will reveal the names of all owners and manner in which title is held as well as outstanding encumbrances and any liens against the property.

Competitive Market Analysis

A CMA is akin to a mini-appraisal undertaken by a real estate agent to determine an indicated price range for a subject property which, in this case, is the seller's home. It is prepared by means of a study of pertinent data relative to similar homes, preferably in the same neighborhood, which have been or are now on the market. Such data is gleaned from multiple listing publications, your office records of past sales, and, if it is in your farm area, from your own records. It is sometimes necessary to contact the agents who listed or sold homes in the vicinity and, possibly, the current residents of recently-sold homes. There are printed forms available to use for CMA preparation or you can design one of your own.

Recent Sales

By referring to a local map and information in past issues of multiple listing publications, you will be able to determine the addresses of homes similar to the seller's which have recently sold. Sale dates should be as close to the present date as possible but, if the market is slow, the time period could go back as much as a year.

You already know the architectural style of the subject home. If it is a ranch, look first for ranch-style homes for your comparables; if a 2-story, that is the model to seek in past sales data. For CMA purposes, you will need at least three homes; in some cases, there won't be three and you'll have to use larger or smaller homes. There may even be times when you have to use similar homes in a nearby neighborhood of equal quality.

Drive by the homes you select to determine just how well the homes and locations compare with the subject property. Consider their curb-appeal (appearance from the street) but keep in mind this could have altered for better or worse when the properties changed hands.

Once you have selected the homes you intend to use as the basis for your study, enter their pertinent data on a columnar worksheet (see Figure 10).

The number of days a property was on the market is the period of time that elapsed between listing date and the date the seller accepted the purchaser's offer (not the date of the close of escrow). It is advisable to contact the agents who listed or sold the comparables to doublecheck sale date as it does sometimes happen that agents will confuse the definitions. At the same time, you can inquire as to the condition of the homes at the time they were sold and whether extra features/upgrades (pool. spa, extra rooms, remodelled kitchen, new carpet, etc.) were included with the sale. Occasionally you will encounter an agent who is reluctant to assist you, or who simply does not remember the details. In such instances, you may wish to contact the home's present owner.

With these facts before you, you can work out an estimate of value for each of the homes sold had they all have been equal, i.e. basic homes in good condition. This is done by adding to the actual sales prices a replacement cost figure for special features that the subject home offers which were not included with the sold properties and by deducting from the sales figures replacement cost of extra features they possess which the subject does not. Estimated cost of any maintenance

WORKSHEET FOR USE IN C.M.A. PREPARATION

FEATURE	SUBJECT PROPERTY	HOME #1	$±	HOME #2	$±	HOME #3	$±
Address							
Type							
Sq ft							
Age							
Lot size							
Bedrooms							
Bathrooms							
Kitchen							
Family room							
Dining room							
Laundry fac.							
Other rooms							
Garage							
Blt.-in appl.							
Landscap./fence							
Extra features							
Personal prop.							
Condition							
Taxes							
Days on mkt.							
Closing date							
Terms							
Sold price							
Total ± adjustment							
Adjusted 'sold' price							

Date of inspection ....

Indicated price range ....

Figure 10. Worksheet for use in preparing a Competitive (or Comparative) Market Analysis. This example can be enlarged to 165% on a photocopy machine to provide 8.5" x 11" forms.

work and materials needed to bring the homes to equal condition is handled in the same way. Estimated replacement cost figures can be obtained from a valuation book.

The bottom line on your worksheet reveals the sales prices at which the comparables would have sold if they had been almost exactly the same as the subject. When properties you have chosen are good examples for the market, the difference in price between the lowest and highest figures on that line should not exceed 5% and are indicative of the price range in which the subject property can be expected to sell.

Current And Expired Listings

In a separate section of your CMA, enter the addresses of competitive homes now on the market, those that prospective buyers will be considering along with the subject property. Note the listed price, condition, special features, terms and days on market to date. If you have not already done so, preview these and then judge how they compare with the subject property and consider where it fits into the indicated listing price range.

The third section of your form will feature properties which came on the market but did not sell prior to listing expiration date. Contact the listing agents and ask their opinion regarding the reason for the lack of a sale. It could be due to over-pricing, condition, a seller who would not cooperate with showings or a variety of other reasons. Compare those, too, with the subject property.

The knowledge gained in CMA preparation about past and present market activity is invaluable when you are discussing a listing price with the seller.

Although you have now determined a "listing price range". you will not be able to pinpoint a figure to recommend until you have toured the home, formed your own impression concerning it and have discussed motivation and marketing face-to-face with the seller.

10

The Listing Appointment

The time has arrived for your listing appointment. You have done your homework thoroughly and, armed with CMA and presentation book, you can set forth with confidence and high hopes.

Some listing appointments are so easy, you'll wonder what all the fuss was about. Close friends and relatives who want to give you a chance to get started, or satisfied former clients/customers who have previously used your services to solve their real estate problems, would not even consider listing with anyone else. Then there are the sessions which will call for every ounce of skill you possess if you want to gain the sellers' signature on a listing agreement. Whichever form your appointment takes, make up your mind to remain calm and maintain your friendly, positive attitude throughout the meeting.

Walk Through The Sellers' Home

Arrive at the prospective clients' home on time. The first order of business should be a tour conducted by the owners. Try to view the home as though you are a prospective purchaser. Carry a clipboard and take notes. Limit your questions to the area you are being shown; in the kitchen, ask if the refrigerator will be left for the buyer; in the utility room, inquire about the washer and dryer; in the dining room determine the sellers' intentions regarding the elaborate chandelier. Watch for telltale cracks or watermarks on floors, walls or ceilings and find out what caused them and any remedial measures taken; later these should be noted on the disclosure form by the sellers. Ask the latter if there are other defects known to them which are not readily visible.

By keeping conversation to a minimum as you walk through you can better absorb what you are seeing. Analyze your initial impression; is it favorable? Note to yourself any inexpensive improvements the sellers could make that would capture a potential buyer's interest. Consider how well the home compares to the ones you used in the CMA and where it fits into the indicated price range.

Interview With The Sellers

When the walk through is finished, suggest sitting down together at the kitchen or diningroom table. These are the preferred places to work because passing paperwork around the table is convenient and the "togetherness" gives maximum opportunity for eye contact. Now that you've seen the property, the sellers will be anxious to have your opinion of its value. Explain that, before making a recommendation, you have a few questions.

Ask the reason for selling because this has a direct bearing on the listing price you will suggest. For example, if the reply indicates that a very quick sale is important and you know the average market time on your comparables is 90-120 days, a listing price at the low end of your range is indicated. Perhaps the sellers want to buy a more expensive home and need to gain top dollar from the sale of the present one. This means that the house must compare very favorably with those currently on the market to justify a price at the high end of the range. If, in your opinion, it does not, point out the differences.

Offer your suggestions regarding maintenance and cosmetic work which the sellers could consider to help the house show well and bring the best possible price. Point out the wonders that doing all necessary maintenance and "spring cleaning" can accomplish. Fresh paint in a neutral, light color, non-dripping faucets, everything in good working order and a clean, uncluttered appearance throughout the home make a world of difference. Tell the sellers about "optical illusions": how, for example, uncrowded, neatly arranged closets seem spacious but the same closets crammed to capacity suggest to the buyer that these were too small for the sellers and would not be adequate for his needs either. Curb appeal is a must which means a neatly-trimmed front lawn free of unstored gardening equipment (or children's toys) and a well-maintained front entry. Very often buyers will spend time waiting on the front porch for the doorbell to be answered or for the agent to get the lockbox opened and will notice if it has not been swept, the screen door needs replacing or the front door has been scratched by the family dog.

It is very important to use utmost tact when presenting these ideas. Above all, avoid giving sellers the impression that you are in any way criticizing their lifestyle. You might cite visiting an unoccupied, new model home as an example and say that most people like to think this is the way they live but, in the actual reality of busy, everyday life, we all know that such immaculate neatness is almost impossible.

Go on to say that, nevertheless, if they could try to have their home resembling a builder's model during the marketing period, and especially when a showing or open house is scheduled, the chances of a sale at a good price in the shortest time would be much improved. Sympathize with them about the extra housekeeping this will entail and suggest to sellers who have children that they might want to organize a neatness competition to encourage family cooperation during this selling period. As you discuss these things, observe the sellers' reactions. You will gain an idea of how cooperative they will be with showings.

Do not suggest that the sellers should undertake major improvements such as room additions or extensive remodelling. This is not the time to go to that expense. If the house really needs this type of work, it is better to adjust the listing price so that the buyers can have the work done to their own tastes.

Net Proceeds

After you have considered all the facts, show the sellers your CMA and go through it explaining how you reached the indicated price range. Then, based on the information you have acquired during your tour and interview, tell them the figure you are recommending as the listing price.

What is really important to sellers is the amount of money they will realize from the sale but many do not know how to relate "price" to "net proceeds". Use a worksheet (an example is presented in Figure 11, page 81), to show them how to get an approximate idea of the amount of money they will receive at close of escrow. Point out to the sellers that, due to variations in fees charged by lenders, escrow companies and other services, and without the benefit of actual verification of mortgage balances, etc., the figures cannot be guaranteed.

Once they understand how to estimate proceeds from a projected price, the sellers are better able to consider how acceptable the indicated listing range is to them and, in particular, your recommended price.

Do You Want This Listing?

You will encounter some homeowners who are very receptive to suggestions you make; their goal is to get their home sold, they have called in a professional and working with them will be a pleasure. Others, however, are not so cooperative and you will already have sensed a lack of rapport between you. Your suggestions have been received negatively and it seems unlikely any will be followed. Further, the sellers have pre-conceived ideas of the price at which they will list their home and your most logical CMA-supported reasonings fail to convince them to list in the indicated price range.

You must ask yourself if this is a listing you want to take. It is both expensive and discouraging to be the listing agent on a property that, despite your best efforts, does not sell due to overpricing, lack of cooperation, etc. It is better to decline and, instead, acquire a listing about which you can be enthusiastic and feel you have a fighting chance of getting the sales job accomplished. Never take a listing just for the sake of having one. It is no favor to the sellers and a disservice to yourself and your broker.

Of course, in most instances you will want the listing and will continue with your efforts to convince the sellers that you and your company are the right combination with which to entrust the sale of their home.

The Presentation Book

Turn now to your listing presentation book and use it as a visual aid while you tell the sellers about your company and your proposed plan of action to find the right buyer for this home.

When you reach the sales contract near the end of the book's pages, you might say:

"This is the form that will be used when a buyer wants to purchase your home. It is a very important document and, later, I would like to go over it with you in detail and answer any questions about it which you may have."

Turn the page to reveal the partially completed listing

This form is merely an outline of general expense items which may be expected by seller when projecting potential proceeds from sale of a property. Due to variations in fees charged by lenders, escrow companies and other services, and without the benefit of actual verification of principal balances and amounts payable to seller's present mortgagees, the figures cannot be accurate and are in no way guaranteed by broker or broker's representative.

ENCUMBRANCES: (1)

Listed Price $ _____

1st mortgage balance $ _____

2nd mortgage balance   _____

3rd mortgage balance   _____

Total encumbrances   _____

EXPENSES:

Equity $ _____

Loan prepayment penalty   _____

Title insurance premium   _____

Escrow service   _____

Notary   _____

Document preparation   _____

Recording/reconveyance   _____

Documentary fee   _____

Transfer tax   _____

Cert. of taxes due   _____

Taxes (preceding year)   _____

Taxes (current year) (2)   _____

Special taxes/assessments (2)   _____

Homeowners assn. dues (2)   _____

Pest Control Inspection (3)   _____

Home warranty premium   _____

Loan discount fee (4)   _____

Attorney's fee (5)   _____

Broker's service   _____

Other: _____   _____

_____   _____

Estimated expense total: $ _____

Projected proceeds   _____

Owner-carry financing   _____

Projected cash proceeds (6) $ _____

FOOTNOTES: (1) Amounts due to lenders will increase by per diem interest since last payments, late fees, etc.; (2) Depending upon closing date, may be pro-rated between seller & buyer (a mythical date could be selected in order to indicate a figure); (3) Inspection report may indicate work required and cost estimate before certification can be given; (4) Applies when seller's terms include certain government loans, for example, or buy-down of interest rate to assist buyer; (5) When applicable; (6) May be increased by the amount of any funds seller has in an impound account with lender.

Figure II. Example of worksheet for pre-listing use in projecting seller's proceeds. Considerations will vary from one state to another; more items or less may need to be included on the form. A standard, professional form for the particular state is recommended for use to estimate proceeds at the time an actual offer-to-purchase is received (see page 6 for possible suppliers).

agreement clipped to the inside back cover of your presentation binder and continue,

"Of course, before I can go to work to find the right buyer, we need to finish filling out this form."

Ask For The Listing

Take out a pen or portable typewriter and begin filling out an Exclusive Authorization and Right To Sell listing agreement form. You may prefer to fill in the easier blanks first to put the sellers at ease and then tackle the weightier matters of personal property and price.

Personal Property

Always be certain that the disposition of personal property is set forth in the listing agreement. Many agents who neglected to do this can tell you some sad stories of the consequences of this failure and how they came to wish they had given this important subject the serious consideration it deserves when they took a particular listing. You might say, for example:

"We talked a little bit already about personal property. You told me that you intend to take the refrigerator with you when you move but will leave the washer and dryer here for the buyer. I am going to write that on this form and, while I do that, perhaps you can come to a decision about the lamp over the pool table in the family room."

It is really important to all concerned--you, the sellers and buyer--that the sellers' wishes concerning specific items of personal property about which controversy could arise be expressed in the listing agreement. Following close of escrow, if the buyers discover when they take possession that the diningroom chandelier is missing that they had assumed was included, you will be the person they will telephone to take care of the problem. You then contact the sellers and they remind you that they told you when they showed you their house the first time that the chandelier was left to Mr. Seller in his grandmother's will and they would be taking it with them. Maybe you remember it now, maybe you don't; the question is, what are you going to do? The only solution at that late date is for you to join the ranks of many other agents who have learned the hard way: advise the buyers to choose a replacement for the missing item and pay for it out of your commission check!

Apart from potential depletion of your bank account, you must think ahead when you take a listing to protect the sellers. Here's another scenario. In the master suite is a pair of handmade drapes which match the bedspread. These were not excluded in the listing agreement because you overlooked them and the sellers assumed that nobody would want to own a used bedspread and would not expect the matching drapes to be left behind either. A month later, you have an offer to present in which the buyer has specified the drapes must remain. The sellers won't part with them because Mrs. Seller's mother made them for her, yet the buyer is determined to have them. Instead of being able to get the sellers' ready acceptance on what is otherwise a very good offer, you are faced with trying to solve a problem concerning who will possess a pair of bedroom drapes! Unfortunately, trivial as it may seem, this can turn into the type of problem that only a skilled negotiator can solve and all too often it can result in a total impasse.

To avoid possible controversy, if a light fixture (or other item) is going out the front door with the sellers, it is a good idea to recommend that they take it down and replace it before marketing begins. When certain appliances are not to be left with the house, it is politic for you to tape a typewritten card to them ("This Item Not Included In Sale") which will be evident to prospective buyers as they tour the home.

Listing Price

When the time is appropriate to tackle the sometimes thorny topic of price, ask first for the figure you want:

"Earlier I recommended that you offer your home at a price of $XX,XXX". Can we go ahead on that basis?"

Hopefully, you will not get an objection. If you do, you might use one or more of the following persuasive suggestions:

1. "We can certainly try a higher price. However, when a house first comes on the market, everyone gets excited about it. If it is priced higher than the competitive market analysis indicates it should be, the chances of a sale are not very good and it will most likely remain on the market without an offer".

2. "Agents are often asked by buyers before they see it how long a house has been on the market. When they are told two or three months, they tend to think there is

something wrong with it so won't want their agent to show it to them. We sometimes get buyers who are looking for a bargain and, when they see a house that's been listed for a long time, they will want their agent to write up a low offer."

3. "Buyers these days do a lot of shopping around and we find that they are quite knowledgeable about prices. Although people who are shown your home will really like it and would want to own it and live here, the majority would not be willing to pay more for it than they would have to pay for a similar home. Yes, I know they could make an offer but some would not either for fear of hurting your feelings or because they do not want to risk another lower-priced home that they like getting sold while they wait for your answer."

4. "We want to keep all the real estate agents excited about your home so that they will bring their buyers to see it. A large percentage of homes in our town are sold by different agents than the persons who have them listed so we consider them a vital part of our selling team. Now, if it is overpriced, while I would still show it myself, of course, other agents may not because they realize there is small chance the people they are working with would be willing to pay a price for it that is higher than they would have to pay for a similar one. I'm afraid these agents would feel they would be wasting their own and their customers' time."

5. "If you did not own this home and wanted to buy a house around here, would you be willing to pay $XX,XXX for this one or would you be more inclined to choose the one at (address) which is $X,XXX lower in price yet is very similar?"

6. "When your home is on the market for sale, no matter how considerate everyone is who brings buyers to look at it, your normal life is disrupted. I am willing to try marketing your home at this higher price but I do want you to realize that we will be faced with a far longer marketing period. What we are really doing is marking time until the sales of other houses justify this price. Do you really want to have to keep your home in builder's show model condition any longer than absolutely necessary? If we can put your home on the market at $XX,XXX, I feel we will have a buyer in the shortest possible time. I honestly believe that the price I am recommending is realistic and reflects a value which is

fair to you, as sellers, and to the family who will buy your home."

As soon as you agree on the price, write it in quickly; assuming all data has now been entered on the form, pass your pen to the sellers and ask for their acknowledgment. (Licensees in California must provide an agency disclosure form to the sellers and get it signed before entering into a listing agreement. This regulation became effective January 1, 1988.)

We have already discussed the reason the signatures of everyone in title must appear on the listing agreement. Perhaps you have obtained this data by now; if not, ask the sellers to show you a copy of the deed or title policy. It sometimes happens that, at the time of listing, all those in title are not present. You will then need extra copies of the listing agreement so that you can leave two with the seller; one is sellers' copy and the other is an extra broker's copy for the spouse (or other concerned party) to sign when he/she returns home. If you find that any person in title resides elsewhere, obtain the address from the sellers and advise that you will send a copy of the form for signature. Mail two copies of the listing to that person together with a letter and stamped, addressed return envelope. In an explanatory letter, request that the forms be executed and one copy sent back to you right away.

In certain States it is a requirement that sellers complete a special disclosure form regarding their entire knowledge of the present condition of the property and other pertinent information. If you work in one of these areas, give your sellers copies of the appropriate form now and offer to assist, if necessary, in filling it out so that this requirement can be completed.

Discuss with the sellers the advantages of including in the sale a one-year home warranty. Such warranties generally cover repair costs for wiring, heating, plumbing and built-in appliances. Quite often a dishwasher is in good working order when the sellers move out but, within a short time, it unexpectedly stops functioning and needs replacement. It is an unhappy buyer who is faced with this circumstance yet it was not a fault of the sellers. The person to whom the buyers will complain is, naturally, the agent who sold them the property. The home warranty solves this type of problem; in fact, quite a number of brokers include the warranty at their own expense to maintain a good relationship with the new owner.

Educating The Sellers

After securing the listing, take some extra time to explain to the sellers what will be happening in the days ahead. You will find that your relationship will be much smoother when working with prepared sellers than with those who are surprised by each new happening that you, the sales agent, take for granted.

Talk about the yard sign and lockbox. Explain that the sellers should not conduct showings for anyone who rings the doorbell in response to the sign but should give the caller one of your cards and ask that they contact you; obtaining the caller's name and telephone number should also be encouraged. Reassure the homeowners about the use of the lockbox.

Go over the procedure which will be followed when showing appointments are arranged and ask if there are any times when the home absolutely cannot be seen. Tell the sellers that a number of prospective buyers will be escorted by other sales agents. Leave a blank sales contract form with the sellers to review at leisure for points upon which clarification from you is needed.

"My deah, this buyer wants your mother's drapes!" (page 83).

11

Find A Buyer
For Your Listing

$\mathcal{W}$e naturally feel excited as we drive away from a seller's home with a signed listing agreement. With a motivated seller and a property that's priced right, we have every reason to be optimistic and it is tempting to mentally calculate the amount of money we stand to gain from the listing. Keep in mind that the house must sell and close before you see a penny; if it goes off the market unsold, your efforts so far will have netted you nothing! Concentrate instead on what you will do from now until the listing period ends to get the job done and make sure there is indeed a payday on your horizon!

Plan a marketing program to include most, if not all, of the following activities:

1.   Enter listing into multiple listing system;

2.   Ask seller for leads;

3.   Yard sign and lockbox;

4.   Canvass neighbors;

5.   Caravan for agents;

6.   Flyers for agents;

7.   Promotion at meetings of agents;

8.   Open house;

9. Classified advertising (see Chapter 12);

10. Brochures for buyers;

11. Mailing to target buyers;

12. Innovative marketing;

13. Keep seller informed.

MLS Entry

Policies of your local multiple listing service will indicate how soon you are required to submit the new listing for publication. It is to your own and the seller's benefit to get it done promptly. Finding a buyer for the home is not a formidable task that you face alone; you have, as potential co-searchers, all other agents who are members of the service.

Normally you will need room sizes and other pertinent data in order to submit the new listing. This is when you will find the checklist useful which you compiled earlier (Chapter 1, To Do List, Item 2). Gather the information at the time you take the listing or, if the appointment ran too late, return next day. Remember to have with you a measuring tape of at least 50 feet or, if you need total square footage of the home, 100 feet is a better size.

Encourage the seller to walk around the house with you as you measure. It is a good time to talk about the condition of the house and repeat your hints on making it show to its best advantage. During this visit, collect such information as where the school buses pick up and drop off the children; days of the week for trash service; and monthly utility costs for past year.

Ask Seller For Leads

The sellers may have friends or acquaintances who have, in the past, expressed an interest in the neighborhood. They are not likely to remember unless you specifically ask about it. It could even be that someone has admired this particular house while visiting them and, if you tell them it is available, you could have a customer.

In the case of a listing that was first offered for sale by its owner, ask for the names of anyone who came to look at the home. By contacting those people, you could uncover one who really wanted to buy the home but did not pursue it for any of a number of reasons: seller gave impression that price was firm; buyer would have to sell present house first and, by then, other one might be gone; or buyer did not have enough money to assume existing loan.   Now, with a real estate professional in charge, price can be negotiated; an offer with an extended escrow period and/or contingent upon sale of buyer's house can be written; and alternative financing methods can be revealed to buyer.   You should be able to overcome any such obstacles blocking the way to a firm offer.

Leave a dozen of your business cards with the seller to give to persons who knock at the door and want to be shown the house and to friends who might know potential buyers.   Ask each time you see the seller if more cards are needed.

Yard Sign & Lockbox

The type of yard sign used by your office will determine how quickly it can be put to work.   A stake sign can be carried in the trunk of your car and set in the front yard before you leave the seller's home at time of securing the listing.   The heavier pole-type signs are usually installed by a serviceperson. Depending on the length of notice required to get this done, you may have time to canvass neighbors.

Different types of lockboxes are used in various markets across the country.   At one time, those commonly used were either opened by key or combination and, although still popular, they are supplemented today by more sophisticated models which an agent accesses, for example, with magnetic card or by dialling a personally-assigned number and inserting a special key.   All of them are intended to protect the security of a seller's home but, obviously, their success depends upon how responsibly they are used.

When combination lockboxes are originally purchased, the manufacturer furnishes all of them set with a standard combination.   Easy-to-follow instructions are included to enable the agent to change it to any three letters of the alphabet.   As a listing agent, you should not only make this change upon receipt of the box but, for maximum security, set it again for other letter combinations at frequent intervals when it is in use at a seller's home.   Keep a record of current combinations of the lockboxes you are using on your listings and avoid using such obvious letter groupings as your own initials, initials of your company or an abbreviation of the owner's name or street name on which the listing is located.   Choose a different combination for each box in use.   You may find it helpful to follow a system when assigning combinations using, for example, names of states and edibles. If the seller's surname starts with the letter M, you could vary the settings on that box among M states, MAI (Maine), MAR (Maryland), and such edibles as MEL (melon), MEA (meat loaf). A combination should never be revealed until you have verified that the person requesting same is a bona fide real estate agent.

Neighborhood Canvass

Visits to homeowners on the same street as your listing, as well as those along adjacent streets, is the preferred method to announce that you are looking for a buyer for Mr. and Mrs. Seller's home. An alternative is to tell the neighbors by telephone using a cross-reference directory to obtain names and numbers. The dialog will be basically the same whether you do this before or after the sign goes up; if the latter, schedule the activity as soon as you can. Here's an outline of how your conversation might proceed:

You: "Hello. I'm Jan Carpenter with Home & Hearth Realty. I have just listed Mr. and Mrs. Friscoe's home at 1010 Acacia and I wanted to tell you a little bit about it. Is this a convenient time?

"Good. It really is a nice home. It has 3 bedrooms, 2 baths and a lovely family room. The Friscoes added a convenient breakfast room off the kitchen, too. Do you happen to have any friends who want to move into this neighborhood?"

Neighbor: "How much is it?"

You: "It is offered at $199,000. I'm going to be having an Open House next Sunday afternoon from 1:00 until 4:30 P.M. I would love to have you stop by and you're welcome to bring friends, too. Can I expect you?"

Or, if an Open House is not yet scheduled, substitute:

"It's offered at $199,000. I'm planning to advertise it in Sunday's paper. Whom do you know who might be interested in looking at it before the paper comes out?"

If the conversation is proceeding amiably, before you conclude it ask another leading question, "While we are marketing the Friscoes' home, it is very likely we'll have buyers wanting to move into this nice part of town who need four bedroom homes. Do you happen to know if any of your neighbors are expecting to be transferred in the near future?"

When canvassing neighbors door-to-door, hand them a business card when they open their doors and, at the end of your conversation, give them a printed invitation to the Open House. Suitable cards can be found at stationery stores with blanks for you to fill in time and date or you can have a supply printed of the sample blank shown in Figure 12. If you elect to handle this canvassing by telephone and there is sufficient mail delivery time prior to the Open House, follow up your phone calls by sending a card to each person with whom you spoke. Write a personal note across the bottom such as, "Enjoyed talking with you today. Hope to see you Sunday." Mail cards, too, to those you are unable to contact.

After brochures have been printed for the listing, mail one to each neighbor with several of your business cards and a short note which might read:

> "Thought you would like to have a copy of our brochure on Mr. and Mrs. Friscoe's home. We talked about it recently.
>
> Please call me if you think of anyone who may be interested in moving to this lovely area."

Open Houses

Looking for a place to spend a quiet afternoon resting? That's just what you'll find yourself doing at your Open House if you don't plan in advance to make things happen! Granted this is a good opportunity to catch up on thank you notes and prepare mailings to your farm but those are only things we bring along to pass the time if the worst happens and nobody comes.

Most Open Houses for members of the public take place on weekends, generally in the afternoon. There is no rule to tell you whether you will get more visitors on a Saturday or Sunday. Sometimes you will do better one day than the other; another time it will be just the opposite. If you live in a resort area which attracts a lot of visitors, Friday afternoons are a consideration especially on three-day weekends. Mondays of the latter, incidentally, are not usually worthwhile as many visitors leave for home early in an effort to beat traffic congestion.

When selecting a date for your Open House, check to see what else is happening on that same day in your community or

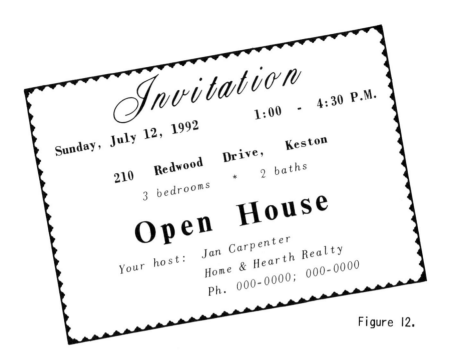

Invitation

Sunday, July 12, 1992   1:00 - 4:30 P.M.

210   Redwood   Drive,   Keston

3 bedrooms   *   2 baths

Open House

Your host: Jan Carpenter
Home & Hearth Realty
Ph. 000-0000; 000-0000

Figure 12.

on national television. You do not want to compete for viewers with the town's most popular parade, nor with NFL's Super Bowl.

Invite Agents And Customers

A successful Open House requires preliminary work. We've already talked about inviting the neighbors. Send invitation cards to apartment tenants in the area, too.

Give the other agents at your office the date and time and invite them to stop in, preferably with customers. Call agents at other brokers' offices who work in the general area and invite them. Tell all agents that, if they cannot get by themselves but would like to send people with whom they are working, you'll be glad to honor their agency. This means that you will be given the names of such parties and you will show them the home when they visit your Open House but, in the event they buy it, their agent will receive commission just as if present for the showing.

Advertising

Remember to advertise your Open House in the classified

column of local newspapers. Writing and placing such advertising is discussed in Chapter 12. Put notices on local supermarket and laundry bulletin boards (remember, please, to remove them on Monday).

Good Sign Coverage Essential

On the Monday prior to Open House, add a rider to the yard sign at your listing which reads, "Open Sunday" (or appropriate day). Drive to the address from different directions and consider the best sites to place Open House arrow signs.

In my opinion, you can never have too many stake signs and I find they generally pull in more people than newspaper advertising. If you find that your office does not have plenty on the afternoons when several agents are holding listings open, it is worth investing in extras of your own. Local sign companies usually have them in stock.

On the day of the Open House, allow yourself plenty of time to get your signs in position. Make them more effective by attaching colored streamers which will ripple in the wind and catch the eye of passing drivers. Tie more streamers and matching colored balloons to the yard sign.

Place a large Open House sandwich board in front of the house. During Open House hours, if you do have a lull between visitors, take a quick drive around the signs. It sometimes happens that other agents who are holding their listings open the same day may have selected the same positions as you did for their signs. If any of them are obscuring yours or lessening their impact, you may need to make a few quick changes. Lock the sellers' home before you leave and post a card to indicate it will reopen in five minutes.

Enlist Seller's Cooperation

When you inform the sellers that you would like to hold the house open on a certain day, do not assume that they know exactly what this entails. On weekends, it is customary to see Open House signs on many street corners but it should not be assumed that the sellers visit those so will know what to do to prepare for their own home to be held open. Spend some time educating your seller and try to win cooperation.

Explain the purpose of the Open House and suggest that a team effort would be really helpful. Some sellers are skeptical and think that the only reason agents want to do this is to get buyers for other homes. If your seller voices this thought to you, agree that meeting buyers in search of houses is a possible benefit to an agent but assure him that the main purpose of investing your time and energies in organizing this marketing activity is to find a buyer for this particular home.

Tell them of the special things you are doing to promote the Open House and tactfully suggest what you would like them to do so that the house is presented to visitors at its best. Point out that buyers hesitate to really look seriously at a home when the sellers are present for fear of seeming to intrude on their privacy or cause hurt feelings with comments or questions. Give them an invitation card so they are aware of the hours and ask that they make plans to be out for the afternoon. The family dog should go with them or, if that is not possible, should be confined. You will be holding many homes open during your career so it is worth having your suggestions printed as a handout (Figure 13).

Set The Stage

Just before Open House is due to begin and the sellers have departed, set the stage. Walk through the home and turn on lighting throughout; open drapes; check that no valuables have been left in view; and turn on a radio at low volume tuned to a station playing pleasant music, preferably non-vocal.

Show off special attractions. Obtain in advance the sellers' permission to have their hot tub turned on, a fire burning in the family room fireplace (unless it's a hot midsummer day) and something cinnamon-spiced baking on low heat in the kitchen oven. These added touches make it so much easier for potential buyers to imagine themselves living here and enjoying the home's attractions. Printed cards are useful to draw attention to special features.

Welcome Each Visitor

Have a guest book open and pen ready, together with brochures giving information on the house (Figure 14) and your business cards. Other handouts might include reading material pertinent to the community and local maps which should either be imprinted with your names and phone numbers of your company and yourself or should have a business card attached. A good place for these is a table near the entry or on the kitchen counter. Some visitors will sign the book without being asked, others will need gentle persuasion.

Home & Hearth Realty
Ph. (000) 000-0000

Help Your Home To Look Its Best
For Showings And Open House.

Experience has proved that homes which are "spring-cleaned" and shown at their best will sell faster than those with a well-lived-in look. The following suggestions are offered to help you present your home to potential buyers in its most attractive light.

Keep grass mowed, edges trimmed, bushes and trees pruned, flower beds weeded, dead blooms removed.

Does the front entry need attention? Visitors wait here for admittance and have time to notice a scratched door, snagged screen, piled-up leaves, children's left-out trikes and toys.

Does the house need fresh paint? View it from the curb where buyers will often sit in their cars and look at the home. Is it time to redecorate indoors? Choose light, neutral shades for a bright, spacious appearance.

Wash windows, clean their coverings. Clear away fireplace ashes after each use and keep a floral arrangement, or live plant, on the hearth.

Closets never seem large enough! Give buyers the impression that yours are very spacious by sorting out the clothes, linens and household items no longer needed and dispose of them. Hang clothes on hangers so that all face one direction with the longer items at one end and shorter ones at the other. Place shoes in neat rows or in an appropriate container. Arrange linens, neatly folded, in the closet.

Keep bathrooms and kitchen sparkling clean and clear the counters by storing small appliances and miscellaneous articles in cabinets and drawers when not in use. Clean out these storage spaces and throw away outdated, almost empty, packages and boxes. Reline shelves and drawers with attractive paper.

Take care of interior maintenance. Fix leaky faucets, sticking doors, etc. Replace any burned out light bulbs, as well as those with low wattage, with 100 watt bulbs.

When your agent is going to hold Open House, please plan an activity which will occupy you away-from-home from 15 minutes prior to the event until at least 15 minutes after it ends. Buyers are more likely to decide on a home in which they feel comfortable about peering into every nook and cranny, asking questions and being able to voice their true opinions. They can do these things when only an agent is present but they would be embarrassed to do so in front of the owners! If you have a dog, take the pet with you or arrange for its confinement. Put valuable personal possessions, such as money and jewelry, in a safe place out-of-sight.

Figure 13. Leaflet for sellers. By leaving out the last paragraph, an agent can also use this as a promotion piece when trying to list homes that are For Sale By Owner (see Chapter 7).

Home & Hearth Realty

12 State Street
Keston, CA 00000
Ph. (000) 000-0000

Jan Carpenter
Sales Associate
Home (000) 000-0000

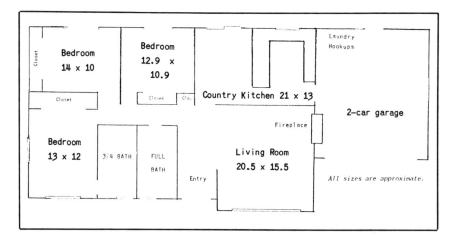

All sizes are approximate.

210 Redwood Drive

Lot size:	102' x 91'	**FRESHLY DECORATED RANCH**
Landscaping:	Trees, flowers, shrubs, lawn (auto. sprinkler)	★ New Italian ceramic tile entry
Roof:	Wood shake	★ Remodelled, sunny country kitchen
Age of house:	22	★ Livingroom has fireplace, new carpet
Appliances:	Elec. range, dishwasher	
Laundry:	Gas/elec. hookups in gar.	★ Fresh paint inside and out
Heat:	Gas forced-air	★ Front privacy fence
Water/sewer:	City	★ Room for pool in fenced backyard
Schools:	Monroe/Montclair/Keston (halfmile to elem., bus to jr. & high)	★ Covered patio
Shops:	1.5 miles	
Public trans.:	Bus stop at corner.	★ Mountain view

⟹ $199,000

Cash or new financing.

Figure 14. Example of a brochure for buyers.

During your Open House, try to greet each visitor upon arrival. Identify yourself, give out a business card and brochure and ask each one to sign the guest book. Make the visitors feel welcome but, at the same time, allow them to walk through the home at their own pace rather than dog their footsteps. When they return to the main area, ask if you can answer some questions for them and try to discover their housing objectives. Quite often it will seem that people arrive in clusters so that you're either alone or trying to handle several separate visitors at the same time. This is another good reason to have the guest book and information material readily available.

If you are trying to get paperwork done or phone calls made in between visitors, keep an alert eye on the street to give yourself time to put paperwork away (or conclude your conversation) before the next visitor reaches the front door. You want visitors to feel important and welcome, as indeed they are, rather than intruders who are disturbing your work.

In the days following the Open House, send thank-you cards to everyone who attended and telephone the people who you feel are potential buyers. If they express interest in this home, the primary purpose of your follow-up is to answer further questions they may now have and encourage them to make an offer; if this is not the house for them, the objective of following-up is to try to help them find the right one by suggesting, and taking them to see, others currently on the market.

Brochures For Buyers

Make up a brochure with complete details on the house to circulate to potential buyers. Choose a format and follow it for each listing you acquire; this method will help you to quickly locate data when asked a question and will discipline you to cover all points when preparing the brochure.

A convenient size to use is 8.5" x 11". Figure 14 is an example of a layout you could follow. You will note that this includes a floor plan but not a photo of the home. Of course, it is best to feature both but, when budget is limited, you can economize by omitting a photo. Instead, take a picture of the house exterior, preferably in color, and have a number of prints made. These can be attached to the brochure when it is being sent to an out-of-town prospect or given to an Open House visitor who shows special interest.

Inclusion of a floor plan drawing is recommended. Buyers

often have definite ideas on what is acceptable to them in this regard and, by looking at brochures that have floor plans, can eliminate homes which are not suitable. Few people can remember the exact floor plan from viewing a home only once so it is very useful to have it sketched on a brochure to refresh their memories.

Mailings To Target Buyers

Your listing may seem an obvious choice for purchase by a certain category of buyer. For example, it might be what we call a "starter home", one that is small and priced so that monthly payments would approximate, or be not a great deal more than, what an average apartment rental is costing in the area. Send a printed letter with a brochure to occupants of local apartment buildings (Figure 15).

Another example would be a nice home in a rural area on a half-acre with one or two outbuildings. Check the zoning and, if appropriate, send information to veterinarians. Put cards on notice boards at feed stores, stables and vets' offices to be seen by animal hobbyists.

Follow up your letters with telephone calls to recipients. It is very possible that you will uncover several prospects for homes whether it be your listing or another property.

Caravan, Flyers & Promotion For Other Agents

Statistics indicate that a large percentage of real estate sales are made by cooperating brokers. If a fellow agent sells your new listing, your personal share of the commission check will be less than it would if you procure the buyer yourself. However, this very good system exposes properties on the market to a much wider range of potential purchasers. It gives you a better chance for a speedy sale and, in slow markets, can make a big difference on whether or not the listing sells at all. Getting the job done successfully will please the seller and win you referral business. Regard your fellow agents, whether they are associated with your office or other brokers' offices, as your valued allies.

Members of the real estate profession realize that we can all win and prosper if we place in number one position the goals of buyers and sellers and work together to ensure that these are met. Other agents, then, may be your rivals as you seek a listing but, when it comes to getting it sold, we are all on the same team. You need their help and they need yours.

Home & Hearth Realty

12 State Street
Keston, CA 00000
Ph. (000) 000-0000

Jan Carpenter
Sales Associate

Home: (000) 000-0000

July 2, 1992

Dear Keston Place Resident:

Enclosed is your invitation to attend an Open House which I will be hosting on Sunday, July 12.

The possibility of changing from apartment living to home ownership may not be one that you have seriously considered. It could be because you feel that monthly mortgage payments would be beyond your budget. Many people do not realize that recent developments in lending practices now make it possible for more of them to qualify for a home mortgage. Interest rates are lower than they have been in years and there are now, in addition to fixed-rate mortgages, special types tailored to suit a variety of budgets. To mention just two of these as examples, one allows the buyer to make a smaller down-payment on a home, another features graduated payments. With tax advantages considered, you could be pleasantly surprised to find that the cost of owning your own home may not be any more than you now pay for rent!

I really believe that this year is a very good time to consider a home of your own. Why not write July 12 on your calendar now and start looking for the right one by viewing the very nice home described on the enclosed brochure? If the date is inconvenient for you, please call me so that we can discuss your real estate interests and I can help you with more information.

If you are among those who find that apartment dwelling ideally fits your way of living, there is still no reason to pay rent. You can enjoy the tax benefits of home ownership with your own condominium. There are complexes to suit a variety of lifestyles. I would appreciate the opportunity to meet and discuss your particular interests so that I can show you a selection of condos which may be just right for you. Please call me any time.

Your friend in Keston real estate,

Jan Carpenter
Sales Associate

Figure 15. Sample letter to apartment tenants. This should be followed up with a telephone call to each recipient to try to discover any who may have an interest in owning real estate.

One learns from experience which agents are really good to work with and those who are not. When you have a buyer and there is a large number of suitable homes of equal quality on the market, ask yourself which ones you are most likely to show to them: those listed by agents with whom you enjoy cooperating or the others? The answer is obvious so do everything you possibly can to earn a reputation as a courteous, knowledgeable and accommodating real estate professional among your peers.

Brochures For Agents

It is generally better to have two brochures for a listing, one for the public and one (or more) for agents. Professional real estate has its own language and there may be information you want to convey to peers that is of no interest to the public.

You may be able to order reprints from your multiple listing service of the brochure which appears in its catalog, or a special version of it. These follow a standard format and, usually, are printed the same color for your listing and those of every other agent in the system. They are adequate for in-office distribution or to give to an agent who approaches you for data about a property but they are not the attention-grabbers you need to stand out among the literature that is handed out at agents' weekly marketing meetings or mailed to their offices.

You do not have to be an artist to make up a better handout. It takes a little imagination, cut-out lettering, clip-art, colored paper and a copy machine. The lettering and clip-art can be obtained at graphic arts stores and most towns now have stores with do-it-yourself copy machines.

The real estate professional will always derive benefits from being a regular attendee at local marketing meetings; when you have listings of your own, it is vital to be there. Arrive early and pass out your brochure every time; there are so many listings on the market and you want every sales agent to be constantly reminded of yours! Change the color each week. Whenever time permits, make up a new one.

At these meetings, if you are given the opportunity to make an oral presentation, never pass it up. It may seem scarey at first to stand up and address a roomful of people but you'll soon get used to it. The audience is not there to critique your merit as a professional speaker, they are interested only in what you have to say about a property for which they might have a buyer. Make notes in large letters on 3"x5" cards to refer to if you are concerned you will forget what you intend to say.

Agents' Caravan/Open House

Encourage other agents to tour your new listing. Perhaps your office has an arrangement for its agents to see the latest in-house listings on a regular basis.

In some markets, weekly "caravans" are arranged by the local Board of REALTORS or by the multiple listing service. Listing agents submit addresses of homes they want included on a particular date and a list of these, in a logical drive-around order, is printed and circulated to all brokers' offices. Agents habitually save these hours on their calendars to tour as many of these open homes as possible. Ask your seller for permission to include the home on the caravan the first week it is listed or, at latest, the second week.

In markets where there is no organized caravan, hold a special Agents' Open House yourself. Plan it for a midweek morning or afternoon and send or deliver invitations to brokers' offices whose agents customarily work the area. The day before your event, phone around these offices with a reminder.

Whether your listing is on a caravan or being held open especially for agents, prepare the home just as you would for any other Open House. Put up directional stake signs and be present to answer questions. Have brochures available. If you plan to hold a buyers' Open House on the upcoming weekend, include that information on the brochure, too, and invite agents to bring or send their customers with the understanding that their agency will be honored.

Consider serving refreshments for agents; coffee and donuts or cookies in the morning, cold drinks and cake or cookies in the afternoon hours, are usually welcomed and cause visitors to linger longer. Ask visiting agents to leave a business card. An easy way to collect these is to offer the attendance incentive of a drawing for a small prize. When you plan to offer refreshments and/or drawing, mention it in your invitation.

Send a short thank you note to each agent who attends and, if you had a drawing, announce the winner. Apart from being a courtesy, the note will remind the agents of the listing. It paves the way, too, if you have difficulty in procuring a buyer, for you to telephone these agents and say, once again, you would appreciate their help.

Innovative Marketing

So far we have talked about conventional marketing techniques but let's go an extra mile.

Exhibit At Community Events

Most communities hold various events which attract shoppers: swap meets, flea markets, charity bazaars, club events, etc. You find booths or tables with all types of merchandise displayed including food, books, housewares, automobile accessories, leather goods, gadgets of all descriptions. Why not real estate? After all, shoppers are people who buy and sell homes!

Next time you notice an advance announcement of such an event, telephone the organizers and ask the fee to rent space. Such fees range from moderate to very expensive. Get your feet wet at one with reasonable costs. Reserve space and plan an exhibit. Photos of your listings can be displayed on large boards supported by easels. On a table, have a supply of brochures covering the properties pictured, together with your business cards, flyers about your company and its services, general real estate information and, of course, a guest book. Arrange the easels and table to form a U so that visitors can enter to look at the photos without being blocked by the table.

Manning such an exhibit can be quite tiring so go prepared. Take along a folding chair, refreshments and wear suitable attire. You'll be on your feet most of the day chatting with shoppers; comfortable shoes are a must and the chair will be very welcome to use whenever you can. If you are doing this alone, you may not have time to take a break all day and will be glad you brought a mini-picnic.

You will meet and talk to a great many people during your day at a community event. Whether or not you find buyers for your present listings, you will make some worthwhile contacts and will have had countless chances to ask that question, "Do you know anyone who is thinking of buying or selling a home?"

Prize Incentives

The time will come when you will have a listing that is not overpriced but is very difficult to sell. The reason could be a slow market with much competition for any buyers; an otherwise nice property which lacks street appeal; or something else. You are doing all you possibly can to find a buyer and you really need help. What can you do to encourage other agents to bring every possible buyer they have to see this listing?

It is natural that any agent will first show a buyer suitable homes listed by that agent's office but, if those are not what is wanted, there is a certain amount of discretion as to what other homes are brought to the buyer's attention. The cooperating agent who procures the buyer receives a specific share of the commission paid by its seller whichever house the buyer selects so you need something that will induce other agents to try extra hard to sell your listing. The solution may be to offer a special bonus.

Special bonuses can take the form of cash in addition to commission, or could be merchandise or a vacation trip. When you decide to use this type of marketing, publicize it extensively. Mail out flyers and brochures every week to agents who work the area. An example is shown in Figure 16. Publicize the bonus at every marketing meeting (and be sure to attend them all) by handing out the brochures. If the format of your meetings allows for announcements by agents, don't be bashful; welcome this chance every time to verbally remind those present about the extra incentive to sell your listing.

The question must be answered in advance as to who will underwrite the cost of the bonus. The seller? Your broker? You? The seller has already agreed to pay a substantial fee to get the home sold so, unless extremely motivated, is unlikely to be willing to contribute more of the proceeds. For this reason, the cost is likely to be borne by you or your broker or be shared between the two of you. This may seem unpalatable but, remember, it is better to receive some remuneration for the work you have put into marketing this listing than nothing at all.

It never hurts to use your ingenuity when marketing your listings. Put your imagination to work and see what novel ideas you can conceive but, remember, these can only be effective if you act upon them!

An Informed Seller Is A Happier Seller

The sellers signed the listing and watched you put a for sale sign in the yard and a lockbox on the door. Just like you, they are filled with anticipation that soon a buyer will come along and free them to move and get on with the next stage of their lives. Treat the sellers always with kid gloves. To ensure their best cooperation, you need them on your side.

Start by sending the sellers a thank you note the day after you list their home. Keep in close touch with them by telephone and/or personal visit (at least once each week) and give them constant reassurance. When there is a showing, advise the sellers of buyers' comments; follow up with other agents who show the property to learn their opinions and their customers' reactions. Give the sellers copies of brochures you prepare for their home.

When it is time to make your weekly report, you always hope to have some good news to convey be it positive interest shown by a prospect or simply favorable comments by other agents. You will not always have this advantage but your enthusiasm and emphasis on marketing plans are a fair substitute. The very fact that you are keeping the sellers appraised of everything that is happening will keep them satisfied that you are not one of those agents who takes the listing and disappears until renewal time. You will be in command of the situation.

Agents who fail to communicate eventually receive phone calls from their sellers demanding to know what's happening. Even if they have been diligent on the job, the agents are immediately placed on the defensive and have to make excuses. Take the positive approach and communicate regularly with your sellers. They will generally be much more receptive to your ideas and even accept more readily your suggestion, if it becomes indicated, to lower the price.

Keep Listing Status Current

When you gain a listing, enter a reminder in your daytimer to take renewal action two weeks before its scheduled expiration date. This subject is covered in Chapter 8.

Even if the property is already in escrow on your reminder date, it is good business practice not to allow the listing to expire. You may believe you have a solid buyer and a motivated seller but nothing is ever certain until escrow has closed. You are in a far stronger position now to ask for an extension than you will be if the deal falls through and you then have to face an unhappy seller with your request to relist.

What is YOUR favorite faraway place?

EUROPE,   NEW ZEALAND,   HAWAII,   BARBADOS?

Fly there when you sell   ...   .

210 Redwood Drive

Three spacious bedrooms, 2 large bathrooms & expansive livingroom with brick fireplace. Italian tile entry hall. Sunny, remodelled country kitchen features new cabinets & mosaic-tile countertops.

Sliding glass door leads from kitchen to covered patio. Privacy-fenced yard offers lawn, plum trees, mountain view.

$199,000

Apx. room sizes: LR---20.5 x 15.5
K/FR---21.0 x 13.0
Bedrms.---13 x 12; 14 x 10.9;
12.9 x 10.9

Lot size: 102' x 91'
Age: 22 apx.
Heat: FAG;
Laundry: Hookups in garage
Appliances: Elec range, dishwasher

Home & Hearth Realty
12 State Street
Keston, CA 00000
Ph. (000) 000-0000

LISTING AGENT:

JAN CARPENTER
000-0000

Figure 16.   Sample of flyer for distribution to real estate agents via marketing meetings, mail, etc., to publicize special incentive being offered by a broker on a listing.

12

The Classifieds
& Other Advertising

$\mathcal{S}$ ellers expect to find their homes included in the classified advertising columns of their local newspaper. The agent who does not run such an ad, at least in the Sunday edition, will have some explaining to do. It is of little use to tell sellers that a sale of their home as a direct result of such ads is very unlikely because the majority of them will not believe you and will privately consider you are unwilling to spend the money for an ad.

Pleasing the seller, then, is a prime reason that the classifieds are so well supported by real estate agents. A secondary reason, yet of equal importance from our viewpoint, is that a well-worded ad will make the telephone ring. The ad will put you in touch with current participants in the buying pool and, if your telephone technique is successful, will provide you with customers with whom to work. Your association may well begin with a showing on the home you advertised but the one they buy is more likely be one of those you show them after you have analyzed their qualifications (see Chapter 14).

The effectiveness of classified advertising depends not only on how well the ad is written but also on the media available in your market and its appeal to the segment of the public you need to reach. At one time, I worked in a large metropolitan area which had two daily newspapers. The morning one was a tabloid, sized right for people who rode the bus to work. The afternoon paper was full-size, perfect for the executive to relax and read at home after a busy day. Most of my listings were resort condominiums, a weekend "toy" or second home for those whose income and interests lay in that direction. I experimented with both newspapers and found that the serious buyers came from the afternoon paper; I used it very successfully on a daily basis. Before I left that market, the afternoon newspaper was sold to an out-of-state owner who made several changes; most drastic was the switch from afternoon to morning publication. After that, the results from my classified advertising hardly justified the cost.

If there is more than one daily newspaper in your market, conduct your own experiment: place an ad in each of them and make it a point to ask callers in which one they read it. Keep a record of these responses as well as the results from the calls. It will soon become evident which newspaper is bringing you the most inquiries, but, most important, is not quantity but quality. Once you have determined which newspaper brings you calls from serious buyers, concentrate your advertising dollars in its columns.

Best Days To Advertise

Next consideration is when to advertise. Sunday should certainly be on your schedule. Buyers know that this is traditionally the newspaper issue in which to find the most homes advertised and where they can expect to find information about which ones will be open for viewing. People planning to move to the area will often subscribe to the Sunday edition of the paper.

Advertisements on Wednesdays and Thursdays will sometimes result in calls from those planning to look at homes during the coming weekend. Friday is a good day to catch the attention of out-of-towners who have arrived early for two days of house-hunting. If you are working with a morning newspaper, you may wish to include the Saturday issue but, if it is an afternoon paper, I have found that a Friday ad is more effective. Least effective are ads run on Monday and Tuesday and, if you are working with an afternoon paper, Saturday.

Advertising Frequency

How often you are able to advertise must, of course, depend upon your budget. My personal preference is to run small ads frequently rather than spend my advertising dollars on big splurges. This policy gives your message a better chance of notice by the most number of current buyers. Your name will gain recognition among those other buyers who are in no hurry but will eventually buy and, meantime, read the classifieds regularly.

As mentioned previously, Sunday should be included on your schedule. In many markets, line rates are higher for that popular issue and, of course, the classifieds are dominated by big ads placed by the franchise affiliates and larger real estate offices to draw attention to open houses and other listings. Don't let these ads intimidate you and cause you to try to compete for attention by taking more space than you need and spending more of your advertising budget than necessary. Big is not necessarily better. The serious buyer patiently reads every ad, big or small, searching for the one which appears to describe the perfect home. In fact, some buyers will tell you that they liked your small ad because wading through the flowery prose of the large ads wore them out and they found your short, to-the-point ad a pleasant change.

Classified advertising is sold by the line, often with a two or three line minimum. Running on a certain number of consecutive days entitles you to a slightly reduced rate per line. Best rates are offered when you enter into a contract to run a daily ad and such contracts can be attractive to a real estate agent if no more than a three-month commitment is required. If you are associated with an active office, it is probable that it already has some type of contract with the local newspaper and you will be entitled to advertise your listings at the preferential rate.

Hints For Writing Classified Ads

The first time you tour a potential listing, carry a notebook and write down your first impressions for future reference. Certain advantageous features will attract your attention: the large master suite with its fireplace and comfortable armchairs on either side; the lovely view from the livingroom window; and the bright, sunny, well-equipped kitchen. On later visits, their impact on you will not be the same because you will be busy checking other data about the home.

When you have secured the listing, add to your notes the fact that the elementary school, a park and neighborhood convenience stores are within walking distance. Ask the sellers what most influenced their decision to purchase this home. Then ask what they most enjoy about the home and neighborhood. Chances are the buyer will be looking for just the same attributes.

There are three parts to a classified advertisment: (a)

heading; (b) body copy; and (c) advertiser identification.

(a) Heading

Consider if you want to use a headline for your ad. It can be typeset either in all capitol letters of regular type or in the more prominent boldface to attract some extra attention. Boldface type, due to size, usually entails a two-line cost but this can be avoided by reverting to upper and lower case and composing the headline to fit on the one line. If you are going to hold the home open, use the headline for the announcement; otherwise, spotlight a feature of the home or try a teaser line. "Breathtaking View"; "Romantic Master Suite"; "Kitchen Delight"; "Walk To School"; "Just Listed!"; or "Hurry For This One!" are examples.

(b) Body Copy

Check a classified ad column for the number of characters included in each line so that you make maximum use of each line and avoid having your words broken up. Some newspapers break words in the strangest places, others simply insert extra white space between words so that whole words stretch to fill the line. Careful planning here can conserve your budget; why pay for four lines of copy (exclusive of headline, if any, and identification) when three will cover the subject just as well? Choose words which will fill the characters available on each line as closely as possible.

Assuming that your newspaper runs 28 characters per line with fewer on the first line of an ad due to capitalization of the first word, consider the following example:

NEWER San Carlos ranch. 3	(25 chars.)
bdrms, 2 baths. Superb view.	(28 chars.)
Easy walk to school, shops	(26 chars.)
and park.	(9 chars.)

giving a total of four lines, versus:

NEWER San Carlos ranch. 3	(25 chars.)
bdrms, 2 baths. Superb view.	(28 chars.)
Walk to school, shops, park.	(28 chars.)

for a total of three lines. If you were working with 26-character lines, the same ad could still be tailored to fit. Observe:

✶✶✶✶✶✶✶ NEWER San Carlos ranch. (23 chars.) ✶✶✶✶✶✶✶

3 bds/2 baths. Super view. (26 chars.)

Walk to school/shops/park. (26 chars.)

Abbreviated words in advertisements are acceptable provided that you do not overuse this practice and that the abbreviations are readily understandable. Substituting a shorter word is a better approach. A thesaurus is a useful aid to writing classifieds; its pages quickly suggest other words to use if more or less characters are available in a line. "Super" could be changed to "outstanding", "nice", "attractive", "lovely", "glorious", "gorgeous", "spectacular", "splendid", "scenic", "stately", etc. Possible alternative words for "newer" include "modern", "up-to-date" and "recently-built".

In the examples above, we do not use the word "home" selecting "ranch" instead. The ad appears under the classification "Homes For Sale" so the reader knows what we are advertising; homes, however, do come in different types and we specify which it is. Few homes are sold without kitchen and livingroom so there is no need to pay for lines to state the obvious. The livingroom's most striking feature is the view; we mention view but it is not necessary to advise here which room benefits from it the most.

The same wording should not appear in the newspaper two Sundays in a row; it is more effective to have a new story to tell. If what you reveal one week does not catch a particular buyer's fancy, your fresh copy the next week for the same house could well cause him to pick up the phone. Our subject house does have a particularly nice kitchen and master suite and we are saving those attractions to feature in subsequent ads.

When buyers are seeking a 3-bedroom home with two baths, reading about a potential benefit to them in the ad can distinguish yours from all the others so far as they are concerned. "Spa" tells readers about an item that comes with the purchase but "Tension departs as you relax in your backyard spa" indicates the buyers' future enjoyment; they can imagine themselves leisurely soaking after a long, hard day.

The market segment to which a particular home will appeal is indicated by the price and its inclusion in an ad will usually limit respondents to those buyers. Price of the property is deliberately omitted from classified ads by some listors who hope to get calls from the entire buyer range. However, by not revealing the price in the ad, the listor may miss calls from qualified people due to their not wanting to risk subjecting themselves to a sales pitch for a home that they may not be able to afford. Familiarize yourself with the requirements of Regulation Z and avoid references in your ad to specific details of financing. General statements such as, "Owner will carry financing" or "Low down payment" are acceptable.

Tell the buyer you want prompt action as you conclude your copy. "Owner needs quick sale. Call Jan Carpenter today!" Be careful with such phrases as "Owner wants offer" as buyers may interpret those words to mean that the seller does not expect to get the advertised asking price. Before using that phrase, or any other that could be read in a way you do not intend, get the seller's reaction.

(c) Advertiser Identification

Rules of your State's licensing regulatory agency plus office policy will influence how your advertisement must conclude. It is very probable that rules require advertising to carry the name of the broker and, if the name of the listing agent is going to appear, that person's name must be the less prominent of the two. Office policy may be to give each listing advertisement an institutional advertising touch by including the company name in large letters to form a block at the base of your ad. Obviously you must abide by State rules and conform to the advertising policies established by your broker.

Length Of Copy

Apart from budget limitations, there are two schools of thought on length for the body of an ad. One subscribes to the theory of the more you tell, the more you sell; in other words, write copy long enough to tell the whole story. The other school believes in using just enough copy to whet the readers' appetites and induce them to pick up the telephone and call to learn more.

Newspaper classified advertising departments will be happy to show you convincing studies in favor of the first school and will recommend that you do not use abbreviated words in your copy. That's only natural; the more lines your ad takes, the better the department's income! The second approach, which also allows more frequent ads to run on the same budget, has been successful for this writer. You will discover which one is best for you in your market by trying them both.

Review Your Advertisement

Don't wait until an hour before the newspaper's deadline to write your ad. Start work on it several days ahead and write a draft. Read it again the next day. Do you still like it? Is it the best you can do? More important, will it attract buyers' attention and cause the phone to ring? Seek the candid opinions of your office colleagues.

You have written the ad as the listor, a licensed real estate agent. Now pretend you are a member of the public working in a totally different career: housewife, doctor, truck driver, retail clerk, etc. Will they understand what you are saying? Are you using real estate lingo foreign to them, or could they possibly read a different meaning into your sentences?

In any newspaper, one should never be surprised to spot the words cute, cozy and cream puff in the real estate classifieds. Don't you often find that "cute" or "cosy" is a synonym for "small" and why would anyone want to live in a home that reminds its listor of a dessert? Remove those three overused words from your advertising vocabulary!

Your local newspaper probably offers telephone service but, if time permits, you can lessen the chance of errors by submitting your advertisement in written form either by mail or by taking it to the newspaper's office. Type it line-by-line as you wish it to appear. When the paper is published, check the ad for accuracy.

Other Advertising Opportunities

Classified advertising in the local daily is by no means the only advertising medium open to you but it is usually the most inexpensive for the circulation offered. One should not dismiss any advertising opportunity, provided that it fits in your budget, without at least trying it to determine how effective it can be for you in your market.

In recent years, picture publications consisting of pages of real estate advertising have greatly improved. Some of these now even include useful articles for the home-seeker and have become very popular with buyers. To justify their space cost, your display advertisement must be sufficiently outstanding to attract the eye of the reader in the short time it takes to turn a page. If the page is turned and your ad has not caused the buyer to stop and read it, you've lost the chance to try to sell him. Go through a few copies yourself and see which ads cause you to pause. Study them and use them as guidelines for your ad layout.

Here are some hints on how to prepare an ad so that it will have the most impact:

1. Use a bold headline;

2. Keep your ad crisp and clean, uncluttered with plenty of white space;

3. Remember that one large, sharp photo of the home's exterior or an outstanding interior feature is better than several small ones. If you have a full page, you could use a dominant photo and one or two smaller ones;

4. To give the illusion of a larger ad to the reader, omit a border.

When you submit your ad for publication, write a position preference in red across the top of the copy. It may be ignored but there is always the chance that the make-up person will go along with it. Request that your advertisement appear on a right-hand page and that it be placed on the page as follows:

Page Size	Position
Horizontal quarter	Across the top of the page
Vertical quarter	Top right, outside column
Horiz. one-third	Across the top of the page
Vertical one-third	Top right, outside column
Horizontal half	Across the top of the page
Vertical half	Outside column

Before you make a position request, check the rate card to find out if the publication makes an additional charge for preferred positions and judge if the "insurance" cost is justified. The charge applies only if your ad appears in the preferred position at your request; if the makeup person puts it there otherwise, regular space rate applies. The worst place for your ad to appear to gain reader's attention is next to the center gutter on a left-hand page.

Weekly newspapers have not traditionally attracted much support from real estate agents because buyers are not accustomed to looking for this type of information in their pages, nor does the cost for circulation realized usually justify a place in our advertising program. There are exceptions, of course, including those weeklies published for communities which are too small in size to justify their own daily newspaper and others which have built up a sizeable faithful readership on their own merits. You may find a very effective weekly newspaper in your area.

Television advertising is prohibitively expensive. In some markets, however, there are opportunities for real estate listings to be advertised on local cable programs. Radio ads, too, generally do not fit into our budgets and are more suitable for office institutional advertising than for specific listings.

Any time you visit another town, peruse publications which include real estate advertising. Quite often the ads will be a little different to those in your local area and will give you fresh ideas.

Free Advertising

Don't overlook any possibility of free advertising. When you get a new listing, type an ad for it on a quantity of cards and paste a color photo of the house to each one. Carry them with you and post one whenever you see a suitable neighborhood bulletin board.

If yours is a unique listing, a house with an interesting history, for example, write a news release and send it to the local newspapers (including the weeklies and real estate publications) and radio and television stations. Attach a note to the broadcast ones stating you are available to be interviewed about the property and can give interesting information and anecdotes about it to their listeners.

Clip Advertisements

Early in this chapter, it was mentioned that one reason for advertising is to please the sellers. This mission will not be accomplished if you don't keep them informed about your efforts! Clip out every advertisement you place when it appears and make several photocopies. Send the original to the sellers with a covering note and file the copies; one should go into a file of all advertising you place in the course of your career, another into the listing file, and the others into a file to be used in other aspects of your work such as listing presentation book, etc.

13

Smile, You're
On The Telephone!

*H*ave you ever answered the telephone and had the caller, a friend or relative, ask if you are tired or not feeling well? We are unable to see the party at the other end of the line but we have a picture in our mind's eye and the expression on the face in that mental picture will depend upon the tone that reaches our ear. Consider mounting a wall mirror near your desk at home so that you can "monitor" yourself during telephone conversations.

When the phone rings, do not rush to answer it. Pick up the receiver after the second or third ring to allow yourself a few seconds to transfer your thought involvement from what you are doing to making a good first impression upon the caller. If you are having a meal or eating a snack, swallow the food and have a quick drink; if you happen to be eating candy or chewing gum, remove it from your mouth. Smoking is another negative factor especially to non-smokers who may be distracted by the resultant irregular sounds in your breathing pattern. Events on the day so far may have been frustrating or discouraging but don't let your resulting mood be reflected in your voice. This call could be the one that will make the whole day worthwhile.

Put a smile on your face and sparkle in your voice when you greet your caller. During your conversation, speak directly into the telephone. People who do not know you well will hesitate to tell you to speak up or say they cannot hear you. Information you are relating about a listing to a possible buyer will not have proper impact. Do not prop the receiver between shoulder and ear while you sign papers, open drawers or otherwise occupy your hands. The mouthpiece will tend to slip below your chin and you will come across to the caller as a mumbler. If the telephone call is about business, it deserves your full attention.

Ask the office receptionist or your secretary not to interrupt you while you are on the telephone except for matters so urgent that a few minutes will make a drastic difference. At home, avoid interrupting your own conversation to yell at children or animals. You want your caller to feel that he/she is important to you, not someone who dares to disrupt your busy life.

The telephone, in a sense, is a Dr. Jekyll and Mr. Hyde instrument. On the one hand, it is a very valuable aid to a real estate agent; it brings us business and facilitates most aspects of our daily life. On the other hand, it can be a colossal time-waster if we allow its Mr. Hyde side to prevail. In the past, most of us have enjoyed long chats with friends by telephone and it is easy to prolong talks even with business associates. At home, if you or other members of your family customarily spend much time on pleasure conversations, you should consider installing a second line to avoid missing business calls. At the office, learn tactful ways to terminate a conversation once the subject has been concluded and it has turned into small talk.

Fielding Inquiries

Advertising that you place for your listings and yard signs with your name rider will result in telephone inquiries directly to you from callers wanting information. Be ready to handle them with the right tools.

Listing Brochures

You will need a 3-ring binder kept up-to-date with brochures on your own listings and those of other agents at your office. Have you previewed the latter so that you are familiar with the "range of products" the "company store" is offering for sale? A good way to arrange the brochures in the binder is to divide them into categories for 2-bedrooms, 3-bedrooms, etc. Within each category, have the properties in alphabetical order by address. Condos can be in subsections in each of the bedroom categories.

During caravans of listings by other brokers offices, you may tour homes of a type for which you sometimes have customers. You could include brochures for such listings in your binder, too, for possible showing when a caller is seeking a property not currently listed by your own office. If you have a fat binder, you may want to make a summary list of the addresses with type of home (ranch, 2-storey, etc.) indicated and file this list in front of the pages for quick reference.

A second tool is a supply of inquiry forms on which to note basic information gleaned from potential buyers who telephone (see Figure 17).

Calls From Advertisements

There are a number of acceptable ways in which to answer the telephone. Choose the words most comfortable for you. Your greeting should include your identity:

> "Good morning. This is Jan Carpenter, Home & Hearth Realty."
>
> "Jan Carpenter speaking. How may I help you?"

The caller tells you that she saw your ad in the Keston Gazette for the 3 bedroom home in San Carlos and would like to know the address so that she can drive by.

Callers from advertisements already know enough to arouse their curiosity about a property. Their call motive is most likely to learn the address or the price. Either query could be

---

Figure 17. Sample of card or form on which to note data about buyers and their needs which may be elicited during an initial phone inquiry.

Telephone Inquiries From Buyers
Name   Phone
Address   Rent/own
Called from: Sign   Ad   Referral from
Inquired about (address)
Wants   brms   baths   dr   famrm   fpl.   gar   yard
Special reqmnts.
No. in family   Ages of children   Pets?
Price range   Area preferred
Employer   Occupation
Notes:
Date

answered very briefly but, if you were to merely give them that information, you would not be very far ahead in your search for a buyer. Instead, try to control and lengthen the conversation with the object of building a rapport with the caller and gaining a showing appointment. You can do this by answering the caller's questions with your own questions. When you ask for the appointment, as indicated twice in the following dialog, do not use words that call for a "Yes" or "No" response, give the caller a choice between one option and another.

Jan: "I'm glad you called me about that home. It is really a nice one. Are you familiar with the San Carlos area?."

Mrs. Buyer: "Yes, I have driven through there several times."

Jan: "Good. This one is on Periwinkle. When you are sitting in the livingroom you can look out across the lake. It's a wonderful view that I think you would enjoy seeing. We have several listings in San Carlos. Are you looking for a three bedroom home in particular?"

Mrs. Buyer: "Yes, we must have at least three. We have a daughter in elementary school and a son just starting college but he comes home for vacations."

Jan: "We have one other three bedroom in San Carlos and a larger home with four bedrooms. Do you mind if I ask your name?"

Mrs. Buyer: "I'm Mrs. Brian Green."

Jan: "It is not very often that we have such a good selection of homes in San Carlos, Mrs. Green. It is a neighborhood where a lot of buyers want to live. I would like to show them to you. Are you available this afternoon to look at them or would sometime tomorrow be better for you?"

Mrs. Green: "Well ... What I really wanted was to get the addresses so we could drive by this afternoon."

Jan: "Yes, I know that was the reason you called me and I will certainly give you the addresses. Is that price range about right for you?"

Mrs. Green: "I think so."

Jan: "All three of these homes have only been on the market a short time. Two are two-storey homes and the third is a ranch. Each one of them is different inside. From the road, it is impossible to get any idea of the view, especially from the master suites in the two-storey homes. San Carlos is such a popular area, and we don't expect any one of these to be for sale very long. Since you are planning to drive out there anyway, why don't I just meet you at one of them so that you can see inside these lovely homes? Or I'd be happy to pick you up and we could all go together. Which would you prefer?"

Calls From Yard Signs

Telephone calls as a result of yard signs are made by neighbors, the curious and bona fide buyers. If you fail to canvass the neighbors when the sign goes up quite a number of the first calls you receive about a new listing will be made by them.

Callers who see your yard sign know very little about the listing other than its style and location. Once you have established that you are talking to a bona fide buyer, you have the advantage of knowing that the exterior appearance of the home and the neighborhood appeal to them or they would not be calling. You now want to learn more about their needs, desires and ability to purchase a home; your immediate objective should be to develop this conversation so that it will lead to a face-to-face meeting. The dialog could follow a pattern such as this:

Agent: "Thank you for calling Home & Hearth Realty. This is Jan Carpenter speaking. How may I be of service to you?"

Mr. Buyer: "I was driving along Magnolia and noticed your sign outside number 223. Can you give me some information about it, please?"

Jan: "Yes, I'm glad you called about it. That is a lovely home which has been very well cared for. It is quite a large home and has an especially attractive backyard. Are you a golfer by any chance?"

Mr. Buyer: "I don't play myself but my wife does."

Jan: "Then she'll really enjoy this yard. It has a mini-golf course set in the big lawn! There is an in-ground spa and a gas barbecue so it is perfect for family recreation. How many are there in your family?"

Mr. Buyer: "Four. We have a teenage son and an ll-year old daughter."

Jan: "This home could be just right for you. It has four bedrooms and 3 baths. The familyroom has a fireplace. Who am I speaking with, please"

Buyer: "My name is Mark Simpson. Does it have a diningroom?"

Jan: "The dining room is part of the spacious livingroom and is conveniently situated next to the kitchen. There is a pass-through opening with shutters in the wall between kitchen and dining. The dining area is separated from the sunken livingroom by an attractive wrought-iron railing.

Mr. Simpson: "My wife probably wouldn't like that arrangement. We have some antique diningroom furniture and she wants a separate room."

Jan: "I understand. Apart from that, does the home strike you as being one that you could be interested in?"

Mr. Simpson: "Yes, I like the sound of that yard and the size is right."

Jan: "Do you especially want to be in that particular neighborhood?"

Mr. Simpson: "It would be convenient for my job--I'm going to be working at Williams Electronics--and I understand there are good schools in that area of town."

Jan: "There are several homes in the neighborhood which happen to be available now. Two of them do have formal dining rooms. Why don't we take a look at those as well as the one on Magnolia? Even though the diningroom may not seem suitable as I'm describing it, perhaps your wife may feel it does have possibilities when she sees it. We could even investigate the feasibility of separating the diningroom and livingroom with a built-in partition. There is another home, too, I would like you to see that has both formal diningroom and large backyard. It is located in a different subdivision but only about two miles from these other homes. Are you free to look at them now, or shall we set up an appointment for tomorrow?"

Your conversation has revealed the reason the caller likes the location which tells you that you can show him homes in other neighborhoods equally well located for his job. He mentioned schools and is interested in a 4 bedroom house so you know he is a familyman with children. The good at-home recreation facilities caught his attention and you can hope that his wife will find a feature of the home of such great appeal to her that it will enable her to overcome her insistence on a formal diningroom.

14

Qualifying The Buyer

$\mathcal{W}$hen a lender qualifies a buyer, he determines the amount of mortgage the buyer can handle by analyzing income, assets, expenses, employment stability and other factors. For the real estate salesperson, the term "qualifying" is more diverse in its meaning. You do need to know what he can afford to buy but you must also determine needs, preferences, motivation, present and proposed lifestyles, etc.

The process of qualifying should not be rushed and should preferably occur during a face-to-face interview; the telephone is an acceptable preliminary when dealing with absent, out-of-town buyers. If you have a choice, meet buyers at their present home; they will be more relaxed when answering personal questions and it will give you an impression of their lifestyle. If they live in a house which they must sell before they can buy, you will be able to estimate the marketing time that will be needed and consider the amount of equity involved. Second choice for location is your office; avoid any setting which is noisy or where there will be distractions or interruptions.

Needs & Preferences

Use a pre-printed form when interviewing prospective buyers (Figure 18). At this stage, you will be a stranger to most of them so begin with comfortable questions concerning their needs and desires. "Needs" are the items that the family must have; "desires" are the frosting on the cake. ("We have to have three bedrooms, but we'd like four." "We have a Doberman so must have a fenced back yard. Lots of fruit trees would be nice.") Inquire, too, about their "don't likes".

Probe as you go along to discover how flexible the buyers are willing to be on various aspects. When told they want a ranch-style home, ask if they would consider a two-story if it met all of their other requirements and was perhaps a better value than a ranch-style? You may be told, "Bill had a knee operation a few years ago and stairs are definitely out", and know you would be wasting your time (and frustrating them) to show alternative styles. On the other hand, the buyers might hesitate and then say, "Well, we'd really prefer a ranch like we've got now". The latter reply indicates that you could include a few examples of other models in your showing tour.

Should the prospect tell you that he doesn't want more than a 20-minute drive to work but you have reason to believe that homes located in that radius will not suit the buyers' budget and/or lifestyle, you might respond: "I can understand that. One or two of the homes I was planning to show you are in a very attractive neighborhood called Willow Glen which I think you'd like. It's about 30 minutes by car from where you're going to be working, Mr. Buyer, but there is an excellent bus service. Should we at least take a look so you'll be able to make comparisons with those that I will show you that are closer to work?"

It is easy for buyers to tell you quite logically what they need and what they desire, although they sometimes have difficulty initially separating the two. Decisions to buy, however, are more often than not made on emotion rather than logic so regard their statements merely as initial guidelines when you consider which homes would be suitable for them. Stay constantly alert for comments which will indicate what appeals to their emotions so that you can adapt your showing tour accordingly.

Ask about family members' vocations and hobbies. Show interest in their replies and try to build up a rapport with these customers. The qualifying interview gives you a chance to win the buyers' trust so that they will be completely straightforward with you in the days ahead and not hesitate to voice criticisms (objections) to homes which you show them.

Motivation

Your time and expertise are valuable so it is important to determine how motivated the customers are and probe for the true reason they are shopping for a home. Are they ready to make a decision to buy now or do they just want to look at a few houses in case they should want to move in a year or so when the last teenager will be leaving home? Are they out-of-towners who like to go around looking at houses to see how they compare with property back home? Some people enjoy passing their spare time looking at home interiors in hopes of finding different decorating ideas. Remember, you are a real estate salesperson, not a tour guide. Showings often inconvenience sellers; it is your duty to disturb them only for bona fide buyers.

The person who is thinking about moving later on is worth following up. Determine the type of home in which he is now living, how long he has lived there and what his thoughts are concerning his next home. It could be that he would be willing to buy now if he saw the right home but does not want to tell you this for fear of being put under sales pressure. If he genuinely does not want to move until the teenager is out of school you could suggest buying now and renting the house until he is ready to move into it. This could work well for the buyer if values in your market are rising and he does not need to sell his present home in order to be able to buy another.

Find out, too, who will make the buying decision. Can the customers make it themselves or must a third party be called in to approve their selection? The latter happens not only when secondary financing is being obtained but also when the buyers want to please their children or feel more comfortable with the blessing of a friend or relative.

You could say, "If I show you a home this week that you like and it meets the requirements you have just given me, will you be in a position to make a decision to purchase at that time?"

During your encounters with customers, whether they are singles or married couples, be alert for clues to which one is the decision maker. If you can gauge this correctly, you'll know which one's objections must surely be overcome. Quite often there is no question in the minds of the principals who will have the final word on which home to buy; they are accustomed to one of them making the major decisions and the other being left to direct more minor aspects of their mutual lives. If one is the breadwinner and the other a homemaker, you cannot assume that the decision maker is the breadwinner.

Date

Name(s) of buyer(s)

Phone   (home)   (office)

No. of children & ages

Present address   (Rent   Own   )

Occupation

Employer & length of service

Hobbies/recreation

REQUIREMENTS   *(if flexible, indicate with ★)*

House	Condo	Townhome	Other	Price range
Style	diningrm	fireplace	-car garage	pool	other
bdrms/baths	familyrm	air cond.	fence	spa

Preferred location

Notes:

FINANCIAL   DATA

MONTHLY INCOME	Buyer	Co-Buyer	MONTHLY EXPENSES
Base inc. from employer			Housing:
Overtime/bonuses/commissions			Rent/mortgages
Other (dividends/rentals/etc.)			Hazard insurance
TOTAL MONTHLY INCOME			Real estate taxes
			Homeowners assn. dues
ASSETS (Estimated Value)			Other
Checking/savings accounts			Payments on loans, credit card & other purchases which will continue more than 6 months.
Stocks, bonds, etc.			
Life insurance net cash value			
TOTAL LIQUID ASSETS (a)			Alimony, child support & separate maintenance payments
Real estate equities			
Retirement fund vested interest			
Net worth of business owned			TOTAL MONTHLY EXPENSES
Automobiles owned			
Furniture/personal property			
Other assets			
TOTAL (b)			
TOTAL ALL ASSETS (a) & (b)	Source of down-payment for proposed purchase		

Figure 18. Typical areas to cover when qualifying buyers. Reference to the standard FNMA Residential Loan Application form is recommended for other questions to consider including when an agent designs a form.

The Right Price Range

From the facts you have been told by Mr. and Mrs. Buyer regarding their wants and needs, you now have some idea of the price range in which you can expect to find them a suitable home. Perhaps you feel it will be in the low $130,000s. Work out an estimate of monthly payment for principal, interest, taxes and insurance using a typical downpayment of 20% and the current average rate and term for mortgages in your market.

> If 30-year fixed-rate mortgages are available at an interest rate of 10%, monthly P+I payment for homes priced, respectively, at $155,000, $160,000 and $165,000 would be $1088.19, $1,123.29 and $1,158.39. Add a figure for insurance and taxes; in this example, we will take $25 for homeowners insurance and one per cent of purchase price for taxes. We now have rounded-off PITI payments of $1,242, $1,282 and $1,321.*

Can these prospective purchasers afford this? At this point in the interview, they should be more at ease and starting to regard you as a friendly, professional person concerned with helping them attain their objective. This will make it easier for you to ask questions concerning their financial position. Tell them that you are about to ask them some questions which may seem very personal but are necessary so that you can show them homes which fit their budget as well as their needs and desires. Assure them that their answers will be kept in confidence.

One of your usual financial questions to buyers will concern the amount they have available as a down payment. You must determine in what form this down payment is currently held: cash in checking or savings; stocks, bonds, mutual funds; a loan promised by a relative, employer or credit union; expected inheritance; or equity in present home. Any one of these can increase or decrease in value between now and close of escrow on the home they purchase; the cash deposits, in particular, could be adversely affected if they happened to make any substantial withdrawals. We all know about the ups and downs of the stock market; the relative may have unexpected expenses so the promised loan would be lower; and then there is the matter of whether or not equity in present home was professionally estimated and if it allowed for sale and escrow costs. At the time of the qualifying interview, you can only use the information given but do remember that it will need subsequent verification.

---

*A variable rate (VIR), adjustable rate (ARM) or other "alphabet soup" mortgage may be more suitable for Mr. and Mrs. Buyer. The traditional 30-year fixed rate mortgage is used here for example purposes.

In contemporary times, it is customary for lenders to require a downpayment of 20%; occasionally it is possible to find 90% mortgages. Most lenders do not expect the monthly payment for principal, interest, taxes and insurance to exceed a range of 25% to 28% of buyers' gross monthly income. In addition, the buyers' total monthly payment for all debts (house, car, furniture, credit cards and any other on-going obligation with six months or more outstanding) must not be more than 33% to 38% of gross monthly income. Although these percentages may be influenced by employment history, income potential and stability, credit history. personal assets and other considerations when mortgage application is formally made to a lender, they are suitable for the licensee's purpose of estimating the price range in which the buyer should be shopping for a home.

Using these parameters, let's consider a case where the combined monthly gross income of Mr. and Mrs. Buyer is $5,000. They have payments of $210, $185 and $60 respectively for car, credit cards and furniture which total $455.

The 25%-28% ratio applied to the $5,000 results in an indicated monthly mortgage payment range of $1,250-$1,400 PITI. The PITI we figured out on homes priced from $155,000 to $165,000 ranged from $1,242 to $1,321. We see further that a house priced as high as $175,000 ($1,399 PITI) could be a possibility.

The second parameter must now be considered. Application of the 33%-38% ratio to gross income of $5,000 gives an after-all-debts range of $1,650-$1,900. Mr. and Mrs. Buyer have miscellaneous monthly obligations amounting to $455 to add to the projected PITI figures. Using our original price range of $155,000 to $165,000, we have $1,697 to $1,776. Even our top purchase price of $175,000 which increases monthly commitment to $1,854 will work.

Before you pass your conclusions to Mr. and Mrs. Buyer, ask in what price range they hope to find their new home. If their range is lower than yours, possible reasons are: they have other purchases they plan to make; they would not feel comfortable with the monthly mortgage payment a higher-priced home would entail; they are withholding certain financial data from you which is resulting in your calculations being incorrect; or they did not know they could consider higher-priced homes.

Mention to them that, from the data they have given you, it appears there is a chance a lender would allow them a bigger mortgage and gauge their reaction. If they seem interested, you can add examples of higher-priced homes to your showing tour; however, suggest that they contact a local lender to pre-qualify. If complete data was not given to you, this will help you avoid wasting a lot of time showing homes that are priced too high for them to afford.

When buyers want to shop in a lower price range even though they can qualify for a larger mortgage, respect their wishes. Keep in mind, however, that if their expressed needs and desires cannot be fulfilled and they are not pleased with what they see, it could be opportune to then show them some more expensive homes.

It is common to find that the house described in needs and desires would be found only in a price range higher than the one for which the buyers are qualified.# Politely explain this to them and suggest that if they are willing to accept an attractive home which meets their needs but not all of their desires, you can show them several possibilities.

There will be times when you will meet potential buyers of whom you are hesitant to ask personal questions regarding their finances. A substitute method is to ask the approximate price they are willing to pay for a home and how much they intend to invest as downpayment; subtract one from the other to come up with amount of mortgage needed and work out the monthly payments on it. Then advise the number and inquire if the buyers would be comfortable with this commitment.

Preparing the Buyer

Before your qualifying interview ends, emphasize to the buyers that you want them to contact you for information whenever they notice a home for sale (or see one advertised in the newspaper) that appeals to them. Tell them that it will help you to help them if you are alerted in this manner to the types of homes that interest them. Assure them that it is quick and easy for you to give them the facts about any home in town, whether listed with your company or another, because you can look it up in the multilist book. Point out that both your office and home numbers are on your business card and you will welcome their inquiries at any time at either place. The last thing you want bona fide buyers to do is contact one of your rivals!

#Remember, the 30-year fixed rate mortgage is being used in this text for example purposes only. It may be possible for the buyer to acquire a higher-priced house if purchased with one of the "alphabet soup" mortgages.

You can make the task of matching buyers to the right home easier by understanding their basic feelings. A major commitment is not one to be undertaken casually and most buyers are constantly nagged by the fear of making a mistake; first-time buyers, in particular, are starting out on an adventure which they have never experienced before. After the qualifying session, set their fears to rest by helping them understand what will transpire between now and the time they move into their new, yet to be discovered, home.

Be sure to prepare buyers for the moment of purchase. Explain that a good-faith payment known as earnest money is required when an offer to purchase is written. Suggest that they always bring a check-book along when you take them to look at homes. Tell them the approximate amount they can expect to submit with an offer so that they can arrange to have funds on deposit to cover the check.

As the qualifying interview comes to an end, give your new customers a "buyer's package" consisting of a letter and offer-to-purchase form. The content of the pre-printed letter, which you should personalize before handing it to them by writing in (or typing) their name and address, thanks them for selecting you as their agent, tells what you will do for them and includes a reminder to call you for information on other brokers' listings. Suggest that they read the offer-to-purchase at home at their convenience and make a list of items they do not understand so that you can explain them at your next meeting.

Language

Choose your words carefully whenever you are working with buyers and sellers. You are accustomed to using the lingo of the business but the customer is not. He may not ask what you mean because he does not want to appear ignorant so a point you are trying to make is lost. Don't put the buyer in this position; use simple words that everyone comprehends. "The date you would like to become the owner of this home" is better than "close of escrow". In addition, use warm-sounding words and phrases. For example:

A "house" is an inanimate object. A HOME is where this family will live;

"Tract" is uninviting as is "development" or "subdivision". Substitute NEIGHBORHOOD and HOME AREA.

"Basement" (or "cellar") conjures up a dark, dungeonlike

image; LOWER LEVEL offers an expansion of main floor living.

Heavy equipment is kept in a "yard" and children play in the blacktopped one at school. GARDEN or OUTDOOR LIVING AREA are more appropriate for one's home.

Disclosure Of Agency

Certain States have laws in effect which require real estate licensees to formally advise buyers in writing in a timely manner exactly whom they are representing in a real estate transaction, the seller or the buyer. Non-compliance with such laws may result in, among other penalties, the principals having the right to rescind a transaction. It is very important to know the law in your State and to follow it to the letter.

Some buyers want to bring their children ...
(Home shopping, page 138)

15

Smooth Sailing
Showing Homes

$\mathcal{W}$hat do you do when you shop for a particular item and discover that the clerk in the first store knows very little about the merchandise offered for sale? Many of us would leave in disgust and find another outlet where the clerks are better informed and eager to be of service. The efficient store will prosper, the other one is a good candidate for an early "going out of business" sale. The same is true in real estate and, because you are reading this book, I know that you do not intend to be the agent who is forced out of the field!

Caravan: Best Way To Know Current Availabilities

Choosing a home is a major commitment for Mr. and Mrs. Buyer. You, the real estate professional, are privileged to have been chosen to assist them and should do all you can to make them comfortable with, and confident in, your expertise and ability.

Keep yourself thoroughly familiar with what is on the market for sale. It is not enough to simply scan your multilist book when a buyer walks through your office door. Set aside time every week to personally preview as many new listings as you can. Make notes on cards as you preview and organize them in a filecard box in alphabetical order by street name. A glance at each card will answer such questions for you as:

What color is the carpet?
Does the house have a good traffic pattern?

Does the kitchen feature updated appliances or
have gourmet cook-appeal?
How is the landscaping?
Is there space for special hobbies?
Any noteworthy view? From which room(s)?

Such notes are invaluable when planning a showing tour. If
the buyer hates green carpet, your notes will indicate which
homes not to include unless you are prepared to sell the idea of
carpet replacement and negotiate whether it will be buyer or
seller who will pay for it; if Mrs. Buyer is a gourmet cook and
Mr. Buyer enjoys woodworking, you'll know just which property
may fill the bill.

In many markets, certain days of the week are set aside for
property previewing by agents from all offices. Often known as
"caravan days", the opportunity is regarded almost as a pleasant
social occasion for some agents; they get together in carpools
and rush through as many homes as they can while they get
up-to-date on the latest chitchat. How much of each home can
they possibly recall a few days later? The carpool route may
even be planned so that it is comprised almost entirely of those
homes at which the listing agents are offering refreshments or a
drawing! This may be lots of fun but is not recommended
procedure for any reader who is serious about getting up and
running in real estate.

The caravan is an opportunity to familiarize yourself with
your current market. Tour with other serious professionals, or
go alone, so that you will have time to absorb what you are
seeing and make those all-important notes. There are so many
properties on the list it is impossible to view them all.
Consider the addresses and prices of the properties on the
caravan list and concentrate on those in the areas of town and
price range in which you customarily work. If any of them are
vacant, see them on a non-caravan day so that you can include
more of the ones that are open today but which you would have
to disturb the residents to view at other times.

Show The Buyers Indicated Homes

Everyone has ideas about the type of home they want and
when we begin working with buyers we determine what these
are and then rank them in order of importance in a
pre-qualifying session (Chapter 14). We also note what the
buyers tell us they do not want; if they are adamant in not
wanting to live in a two-story home, or one in which the
kitchen is reached by walking through the dining room, respect
their wishes. To show them such homes would not only be a

waste of your time and their time but would suggest to the buyers that you either did not listen or do not know your merchandise.

Homebuyers usually have a limited amount of time to find the property they desire. It is up to their agent to start a showing tour with homes which match their expressed needs, desires and price range and be able to answer questions about these properties. Of course, it may be necessary to amend our concept of the type of home they will choose as we get to know the buyers better.

Planning A Showing Tour

In the mid to late 1970s, a "hot" market period, I remember there were brokers who trained their salesmen to show no more than three properties. After viewing those, a buyer who was not ready to sign on the dotted line, was labelled "not serious" and cut loose so the salesman was free again to work with others. Times have changed and there are few who subscribe to that philosophy now.

Buyers who make their decision after touring a reasonable number of available homes, are more likely to be satisfied and you will not have to contend with "buyer's remorse". (That is the peculiar disease that fills the waiting period between offer and acceptance when Mr. and Mrs. Buyer wonder if they did the right thing or were too hasty and should have looked further.) What constitutes a reasonable number? The answer, if you properly qualified the buyers regarding motivation, is as many homes as it takes to find the right one. Of course, if this turns into a marathon of homes with no interest indicated, it is safe to assume that you are not showing the right homes. Stop the tour, sit down quietly with the buyers, go over again their needs, desires, etc., and then remedy what you are doing wrong by changing the type of homes and/or areas on your tour.

The smoothest tours are those that can be planned in advance. In the scenario in this chapter, your buyers are from another town, you have pre-qualified them and know their tastes, needs and timetable for moving. They have advised you that they will be visiting on a certain date and would like to look for their new home. Find out how much time they will have during this visit to devote to looking at homes and if they intend to make their decision based on what they see this time or, if necessary, will return before their anticipated moving date, to look further. When a family is moving from another town, it is important to them to have their next permanent residence already purchased; your buyers will probably tell you they want to find the right property as quickly as possible.

Study current market availabilities and refer to your caravan cards to select homes which appear to meet your buyers' requirements. If you have been given sufficient advance notice, preview any that you have not already been through. Plan a tour featuring the top five or six homes which you believe will appeal to this family.

Anticipate buyers' questions about each home you plan to show, its immediate neighborhood and life in your city. Have complete data for all the homes on your tour even when they are not your own listings. Call the listing agents and get pertinent data. Ask for any additional information that may be helpful to you and your buyers. There may be features about the house that are not readily apparent; the seller may be planning to include certain items which one would not expect (or vice versa); painting or appliance replacement may be scheduled; a particular area of the garden may be glorious in springtime. These facts add to your own knowledge and enable you to give better service to client and customer alike.

A common question you will be asked, especially when a home is of serious interest to your customers, is what prices similar homes have brought. Be prepared with recent comparable sales for each property on your showing tour. Many customers are cost-conscious and may want to know the amount of the annual taxes and utility bills; if you are the listing agent, you will already have obtained this information from the seller. If the seller has not kept a record, contact the local utility companies which, quite often, are willing to quote the past year's high, low and average figures to real estate agents over the telephone.

It is reassuring to a buyer who is making a major home-buying decision to be working with an agent who has done his homework and can give accurate on-the-spot responses to pertinent questions. If you are asked questions you cannot answer, be honest and admit this rather than taking a guess. Say that you will obtain the information as quickly as you can.

Decide the order in which you want to present your Top Six homes to the buyers; it can be effective to place the home you consider your best bet in third or fourth position on the tour. Prepare a routing sheet for your own quick reference and, if you use combination lockboxes in your market, note the codes lightly in pencil (be sure not to leave the sheet lying around in your car or in one of the homes) and erase them after the showings.

Mark on a map neighborhood features of interest which could easily be driven by as you go from one house to another. It is useful to show to buyers who are unfamiliar with the area so they can see how conveniently shopping, schools, churches, recreation, etc., are located to the homes you will show them. Do not mark the homes on the map now, however, postpone that until you arrive at each one; the reason for this will be explained later in this chapter.

Prepare a fact sheet for each home (see Figure 19) and make enough photocopies so that you and each buyer going on the tour will have one for reference purposes. If there is not sufficient time to prepare these, substitute brochures. Fact sheets are preferred because the same information can be found in the same position on the pages for each property which simplifies comparison when it is time to make the buying decision.

Gaining Admittance To Homes

When showing property, you and your customers may be admitted to a home by its resident, or by means of a key obtained either from listing agent's office or taken out of a lockbox. Try to arrive on time for your appointment if the resident is expecting you; if circumstances prevent punctuality or necessitate cancellation, telephone him/her. Whether the listing is your own or another agent's , future showings will be much easier if the resident is treated with consideration.

The collection of keys from other brokers' offices is best done during the hour prior to your appointment with the buyer. Making stops at listing agents' offices when you have your buyers with you (unless directly on your route) is an imposition on the customer's time. Return the keys immediately after you leave the customers.

There are two types of lockboxes in common use, the keyed and the combination. If your market uses keyed lockboxes, you should take every precaution to ensure that your key does not get lost or used by anyone else.

As you organize your showing tour, in markets where combination lockboxes are utilized, you should telephone the listing broker's office, properly identify yourself and office, and give date and approximate time you wish to show the listed home. Upon verification that you are who you claim to be, you will be told the combination of the lockbox on the home you intend to show. When the time comes to dial the combination, stand so that you are blocking sight of the box from your

HOME TOUR RECORD

Home & Hearth Realty

12 State Street
Keston, CA 00000
Ph. (000) 000-0000

Agent

Home   Phone

All figures are approximate only and not to be relied upon. Please request verification as needed.

Price

Assumable loan balance

New financing required

Seller may assist   Yes   No

Address

Style   Age

Bedrooms   Baths

Schools: Elem   Jr. High   High

Apx. room sizes: Diningrm   Familyrm

Livingrm   Kitchen

Kitchen appliances

Fireplace   Air cond.   Roof   Floor coverings

Garage/parking   View   Window coverings

Laundry fac.   Heat   Water   Elec.   Gas   Sewer

Lot size   Fence   Landscaping

Patio   Deck   Pool   Spa   Sprinkler

Distance to shopping   & public transportation

Bedroom 1   Bedroom 2

Bdrm 3   Bdrm 4

BUYER'S NOTES:

Figure 19. Sample fact sheet to prepare for buyer's use during a home showing tour. A similar form, with appropriate spaces for information on the facilities of the complex, amount of homeowner's association dues and items it covers, can be utilized when showing condominiums.

customer to protect the security of that home.

Home Shopping With Children

Searching for a new home is a serious business. Some customers, often the ones who are involved in a job transfer, may regard it as a necessary chore; first-home buyers and those moving up into a bigger or more expensive home look upon it with anticipation. Others, who may be empty-nesters or in reduced circumstances, may approach it with a feeling of sadness. Whatever the motivation, you can turn the search into a pleasant experience.

For starters, consider the customers' comfort. It is not necessary to own a car just off the showroom floor but the one you drive should be spotlessly clean both inside and out and completely uncluttered. Drive steadily and observe the speed limit. Watch the time; depending upon how long your tour is taking, ask if your customers would like to stop for coffee or lunch.

Showings are usually smoother if the customers do not have to bring their young children along. A list of reliable babysitters is a good real estate sales tool and it may even be worth it to you to offer this service at your expense. Even teenagers soon get bored with looking at houses; for those who accompany their parents from out-of-town, your suggestions of more interesting local activities for them to enjoy while their parents are seeing homes may be welcomed.

Some parents want to bring their children and include them in their homebuying decision. To keep these youngsters entertained, carry a box in the trunk of your car filled with small toys, books and games for various ages. Actually, children can sometimes be an asset to you in making the sale; they quickly become emotionally involved with a home's features and tend to be quite verbal about their likes and dislikes. This may encourage the parents to more readily express their own opinions.

The Tour Begins

Your attitude is very important. Regardless of how you feel that day, be cheerful; no matter how many objections you have to deal with, or how many homes you end up showing, keep smiling. In previewing, you set the stage, became familiar with your props and memorized your lines. Now it is time to assume your imaginary role of actor or actress and take your place at center stage.

The curtain rises as you approach the street where the first of your Top Six homes is located. Tell your customers a little about the home they are about to see and drive slowly so that they can look at the neighborhood. Stop in front of the home before turning into the driveway to give them a chance to appreciate its style and landscaping.

Before you get out of the car, give a copy of the home's fact sheet to Mr. Buyer, one to Mrs. Buyer and keep the third yourself. Point out the space left on the sheet for them to make notes and comments and offer pens or pencils for their use.

Do not hand your fact sheets en masse to the buyers when you meet. It could well be that House No. 3 on your list will be the one they'll love and want to own but, if they know you have planned showings at six homes, chances are they will postpone any decision until they have toured them all. You then run the risk of having another of your selections appeal equally to them and will be faced with the difficult task of getting them to choose between the two. This, in turn, can lead to the time-consuming "think it over" objection. It is for this same reason that we earlier marked on the map neighborhood conveniences but not the homes we have selected.

Plan ahead how to guide your customers through each home to demonstrate the convenience of its floor plan. Open the door and, even if you do not expect anyone to be inside, call out "Anybody home?" to be sure it is indeed empty. Step back outside and allow your customers to enter in front of you. First impressions are important so watch for signs of their reactions. For the initial walk-through, suggest which room to enter, then the next, and so on through the house.

Don't rush the walkthrough. Let it be a relaxed stroll with the customers' degree of interest setting the pace. Pause in each room long enough for them to properly see its potential. If the drapes are closed, open them (and remember to close them up when the showing is finished). Give them time to discover for themselves features which are of special appeal to them and visualize how their furniture would fit in the room. Before moving on to the next one, if there is something they seem to have overlooked, bring it to their attention.

Do avoid stating the obvious, i.e. "This is the kitchen." More informative, as your customers are looking at the room, would be, "You don't have to be too concerned about running out of milk in this kitchen. Tom's Grocery Store is just a block away and it's open every day from 7 until midnight." Or, "Mrs. Buyer, the seller is planning to leave her Farberware rotiserie.

She said you can cook the best barbecued chicken in this oven with it."

People tend to be a little uncomfortable walking through a stranger's home. Put them at ease by sitting down for a minute in the livingroom or at the breakfast nook in the kitchen. This gives a better "feel" than simply walking through. Tell them to pretend this is their own home and to feel free to look inside closets and kitchen cabinets. If there are doors to the outside from livingroom, diningroom or kitchen and it is a nice day, open them so that the customers can go outside, too. (Be sure that such doors are locked again before you leave. It's easy to forget them.)

It is not necessary for you to keep up a continuous flow of sales talk or conversation. Keep quiet and allow the customers to make comments to each other or ask you questions. What you hear may help you close the sale.

Once you have been through the house with your customers, you may want to suggest that they go through it again more leisurely. Do not dog their footsteps but be nearby so that it is easy for them to ask you questions (and as a security measure if you do not know them).

When everyone is seated in your car after looking through the home, before you start the engine ask them to jot down their impressions. You might suggest they give the house a grade from 1 to 10 based on how closely they feel it meets their needs and desires. Not only does this serve to help the buyers remember what they like and dislike about each one you show them, but it gets them very involved and can be most informative to you.

Objections cannot be answered when you don't know what they are. By filling in their comments on the fact sheets, the buyers make it easy for you to uncover them. If you gain the impression that your customers are not very interested in the home they have just seen, simply listen to their comments. It will tend to discourage them from verbalizing their feelings at the next stop if you try to overcome objections on a house that they are unlikely to purchase. Instead, remember what they have said; it may help you when the time comes to close the sale on the right home.

After the customers have toured Home No. 2 and jotted down their impressions, ask them to compare its pros and cons with the first home. Which of the two do they prefer? These mini-decisions as you progress from one house to another will help them make their ultimate buying decision.

The 100% perfect home which contains the exact floor plan and every feature your customers have specified and none of the characteristics to which they object is probably yet to be built. Even the most carefully-considered selection of homes will have its plus and minus factors. Prepare the buyers for these as you drive along. You might say, "Our next home is on Lavender Lane. Its garage is not attached but there is a breezeway from it to the kitchen which is sunny and very well designed for someone who enjoys cooking as much as you do, Mrs. Buyer. In addition, it has a really large family room which would be perfect for your pool table, Mr. Buyer. I definitely feel this home is worth seeing."

Subsequent Tour

Your top six homes are the ones that you believe will please your buyers. Probably you are right. However, you could be mistaken. Learning that fact after you leave the sixth home could be a disaster. Your buyers have no time to waste during their brief trip while you return to your office and start over from square one. You must be prepared to handle this eventuality. Have facts ready, and tentative appointments made, to show six more properties.

Before you begin touring those, however, suggest a refreshment break. If you can do so tactfully, leave the buyers at a restaurant or their motel so that you can use the time to review your buyers' objections to the first six properties. Perhaps these objections have revealed facts not previously known to you that may make the homes on your back-up tour inappropriate. Consult your caravan cards and catalog of available properties so that you can quickly come up with a substitute back-up tour and use a pay-phone to make appointments. Telephone, too, to either confirm or cancel the tentative appointments you made for the original backup tour. Your courtesy will be appreciated.

Rejoin your buyers and explain that the homes they are about to see have been selected based on the new information you have learned from them gathered during the preceding tour. As you enter the livingroom of a home in the next group, you might say, "I'm showing this home to you now because I believe that a nice view is more important to you, Mr. and Mrs. Buyer, than having a large livingroom. Don't you agree that the view from both the livingroom and master suite here is very special?"

Answering specific questions on homes included in this phase of your showing tour may be more difficult for you. Try to get on-the-spot answers to specific questions, if necessary, by phoning the listing broker's office from the house.

When you know your "merchandise" well and completely understand your buyers' qualifications, it is easy to select the right properties and enjoy smooth sailing showing homes.

For Sale By Builder

There are certain buyers who will tell you they could never be happy with anything but a brand-new home. In addition, when you are working with buyers from another town, you could be driving them to selected homes you believe will please them and they notice a builders' development en route and want to look at the new homes. If you do not accommodate their wishes, you know exactly what will happen: they will not buy anything you show them without first going (on their own, if necessary) to see what the builders are offering. Be prepared to help those who are interested in new construction.

You should make it a point to caravan everything in your area which is offered for sale by the builder and keep a supply of builders' brochures in your files. Even if you do not have occasion to show any of their homes, sometime in the future you may list one for resale and those brochures are then a great source of information. Apart from the need to be familiar with all product on the market, it is important to you and your broker to know whether or not a particular builder will pay commission if you are the procuring cause on a sale of one of his properties. This varies with the builder and the times: some will pay a certain percentage of the sales price, others only a referral fee; and there are those who do not offer any compensation at all. When there are lots of buyers, one can expect to find that builders want their own personnel to handle the sales; when times are tough, the tendency is to offer good compensation and even encourage agent participation in sales by hosting preview parties with very tempting refreshments. Obviously, then, you need to know the current situation when buyers inquire about new construction.

Spend a little time getting to know builders' sales personnel. Quite often, an agent simply introduces the buyer to a member of the staff and that person will handle the showing either with you present or without, depending upon policy. Do not be surprised to learn that the staff member will also write up the purchase offer and that it will be done on a special form provided by the builder.

16

Closing The Buyer

$\mathcal{T}$here are a variety of techniques favored by agents to close a sale. If you try to memorize them all, you may find yourself a "jack of all trades and master of none". More effective is to become proficient at the ones with which you feel most comfortable. Practise them alone in front of a mirror or by asking someone else to play the role of buyer. Turn on a tape recorder so that you can listen later and hear yourself as others do. This will help you to improve your performance and, once perfected, you can play the tape as a quick refresher course on the days when you have showing appointments; play it while getting dressed, having breakfast appointments or en route to work in your car.

Watch for revealing clues during showings that will indicate a certain home has captured the buyers' attention. Mrs. Buyer is opening all the kitchen cabinet doors, Mr. Buyer is spending a lot of time in the garage, teenage daughter has fallen in love with the corner bedroom, Junior has discovered the basketball hoop. This family which had merely made a few polite comments in the other three houses you showed them today has come to life and you are busily answering questions. Listen, Mrs. Buyer is asking her husband if the piano would look better in the livingroom or family room. Your hopes are rising .... but now the objections begin. Don't despair, rejoice! This is yet another clue which indicates that these people are seriously interested.

Handling Objections

An objection is a cry for help. People dislike or fear making decisions of any kind; to commit to purchase a house with its accompanying mortgage and maintenance responsibilities is tough indeed. Your customers really like this home but it is not easy for them to acknowledge this fact and act positively to carry it to its logical conclusion. They are apprehensive that to commit would risk a mistake they might regret so, instinctively, they fight to avoid it. It is time to stall and they look for anything about which to raise objections; they are buying time to postpone the big decision. You can help them through this phase by asking questions concerning their impressions of the home that they will answer affirmatively; this allows them to reinforce their belief they have found the right home for their family.

Some of the objections, of course, are not trivial and must be overcome. How should you handle them? As usual in real estate, you must be fully prepared. When you have previewed the homes you are going to show, and know the needs of your buyers, you can anticipate certain objections that will arise. Either cover these in your initial showing of the home or be ready with convincing answers when the objections are voiced.

Always remain calm and never be drawn into an argument. You want these people to consider you a friend, not an adversary. There is no reason for you to feel on the defensive--after all, this is not your home to defend! Nor do you ever want your response to an objection to place the buyer on the defensive. No matter how much you disagree with, or consider unreasonable, what is said, if you argue with buyers, they will feel compelled to convince you they are right and you will soon lose rapport.

The public in general still tends to view the real estate agent as being grossly overpaid. If you allow any feeling of animosity to develop between you and buyers, you run the risk of some of them deciding to "punish you" by going to one of your competitors. In fact, if the home you get into an argument over is listed with another company, you could find later that the agent whose name is on the sign in the front yard was called in and made the sale!

When faced with an objection which could easily turn into an argument, skirt it. Use the feel/felt/found technique: "It is easy to see why you may FEEL that way. Other home shoppers have FELT the same. They have also FOUND that homes in this special neighborhood do have the big advantage of ......"

Listen carefully to each objection and be sure you understand what the buyers are really saying. If you have a doubt, clarify with a question of your own. The buyers' problems are yours to solve and you'll be able to do this better if you comprehend their point of view. Whatever the objection, if you feel it is a serious one, handle it and get the buyers to acknowledge their satisfaction with your response by asking a question that needs an affirmative reply. Allow them to answer before moving on to any other topic. Regardless of the length of the pause in conversation, do not attempt to fill the silence yourself.

Be sympathetic with the buyers' feelings and try to respond to their remarks with a positive statement to help them overcome their own objections. For example:

Buyer: "There is quite a lot of traffic on this street. Living here would be noisy."

You: "I can see why you would have that impression. It's quarter after five so people are coming home from work. I showed this house to another couple yesterday morning and it was very quiet and pleasant."

Remember that not every objection needs an answer. In the home under consideration, it is obvious that the livingroom has been freshly painted but there are a few odd marks around the edges of the ceiling which did not get wiped off when the paint brush strayed. The customer says that whoever did the work did a poor job. No comment by you is necessary. However, if the room has not been painted and the customer says it needs it badly, you could say, "Yes, it does. Wouldn't it be great to have this room painted to your own tastes?" When they agree it would, continue, "This home really seems to have all the features you told me you want. Shall we write up an offer which takes into consideration the cost of repainting?"

An objection may be raised which you know is bothering the buyer and needs to be overcome but you need a few minutes to consider the best way to do so. Rather than tackling it then and probably not doing a good job, buy some time by acknowledging the objection non-commitally (i.e. "Yes, I see what you mean"). Try to temporarily distract the buyer's attention by moving to another room or raising a different subject. Think about the best answer and be ready when the objection is repeated. If it is not voiced again after a reasonable time and you still haven't closed the buyer, raise it yourself and give your considered response.

Be prepared with remodelling ideas. Perhaps Mrs. Buyer objects to the small kitchen but likes everything else. If it happens to be adjacent to a family room, you might suggest the possibility, if structurally feasible, that the wall between them could be removed and a breakfast bar/room divider installed. This would not only create an illusion of more space but would enable the cook in the kitchen to converse easily with persons in the family room. When a formal diningroom is next to the kitchen, a pass-through cut into the dividing wall can help solve the problem.

Contingency Closing

Perhaps the buyers have a particular objection which seems to be the major barrier between them and the commitment to purchase this home. Using the small kitchen example again, Mrs. Buyer is enthusiatic about your suggestion of opening it up to the family room but Mr. Buyer is dubious about potential cost of the work and whether it would be structurally feasible.

Paint a word-picture for them. Say: " Let's pretend this wall is gone and we are looking at an attractive breakfast bar between kitchen and family room. You, Mrs. Buyer are in the kitchen cooking dinner but can keep an eye on the children in the familyroom to be sure they're doing their homework. Mr. Buyer, you're relaxing by the fireplace with your evening newspaper and you come across a news item you want to share with your wife. You don't have to get up and walk into the kitchen because you can easily see and hear each other. Wouldn't that be really convenient for you both?"

When they agree that it would be, ask, "As I understand it, then, if this wall was gone, this would be the home you would choose. Am I correct?" Since the wall is in place, chances are that if everything else about the home has pleased them, they will feel safe in giving you an affirmative answer.

Close by telling them that you would really like them to be able to move into this home because it does seem to be perfect for them. Suggest that you write up an offer to purchase which includes the provision that they have the right to have up to three building contractors inspect the kitchen, advise on the feasibility of removing the wall and give them estimates of cost involved. Assure them that if it should prove to be impossible, or the estimates are more than they are prepared to pay, they then have the right to cancel their contract and their earnest money will be returned to them.

The advantage in getting them to make this commitment is that during the waiting time to get the estimates, you can keep in close touch with your buyers and reinforce all the positive aspects of this home. Having had the contract accepted by the seller and in force for the time it takes to get the contractors out, the buyers are likely to become mentally committed to the home. Even if the kitchen project should not be feasible, they may be willing to proceed with the purchase rather than begin the search all over again.

If the remodelling is feasible but too expensive for them to have done at the present time, you might point out that it is something they can plan as a future project. Should you be faced with buyers who would exercise their option to void the contract due to remodelling expense, try one more tactic. Suggest to the buyers that a new proposal be written up for seller's consideration which reflects a price reduction. You owe it to the seller to give them this one last option to sell their property to these particular purchasers.

You can use this contingency closing to overcome any objections that require expertise from other professions. It is also used when buyers need approval from a third party, time to review documents or must approve something else before they actually are committed to the purchase. For example, they may be unwilling to sign an offer to purchase without first visiting the local school and talking to the principal to satisfy themselves the curriculum is what they desire for their children. Whatever the problem is, write up your contract with a contingency to cover it and assure the buyers that this does give them the right to cancel their offer if the outcome of the action called for makes it necessary, or they deem it advisable, to do so. Whenever you write a contract with a contingency, include a time limit. For example:

> "This contract is contingent upon purchasers' approval of curriculum at Keston Elementary School. Purchaser agrees to notify seller in writing no later than (date) if school is not approved and all monies hereby receipted for shall be returned to purchasers. If written notice is not received by date specified, all parties hereto shall regard this contingency as having been waived."

For more information on contract contingencies, refer to the "Additional Provisions" section of Chapter 17

Price Objections

"The price of this house is too much!" says Mr. Buyer. Ask the reason he feels this way. Help him to understand how the price was established by telling him of comparable sales in the neighborhood.

If Mr. and Mrs. Buyer are presently renters, ask them if they expect rents to increase or decrease in the next XX years (XX representing the current term of available mortgages). Realistic buyers will anticipate increased rents and you can point out that, by moving out of their rental and into this home, they are "locking in their rent" in the form of a mortgage payment for that number of years.

Agents with a working knowledge of Federal and State tax regulations can make a correlation for the buyers between the rent they are now paying each month and what their monthly mortgage payment would be when homeowner tax benefits are considered. For example, if the buyers' Federal tax rate is 28% and State rate is 11%, you would apply a reciprocal rule of 61% [100% minus (28% + 11%) = 61%] to their present rent of, say, $795 to illustrate that the rent equates to a house payment of approximately $1,300 [$795 divided by 61% = $1,303.28].

Positive Answers

When you have the impression that a house is of interest to your customers, help them come to a buying decision. Use appropriate questions for them to answer in the affirmative and so vocalize their approval of the home's features and suitability for their needs.

"This is an extra large garage, Tom. Will it give you the space you need for your woodworking hobby?"

"Nancy, don't you feel that your teenager will love having that downstairs bedroom with its private entrance from the outside?"

"Tom, since you often work at home, wouldn't that small room off the front hall make a perfect office for you?"

"You said you enjoy canning, Nancy. Don't you think you could have a great time here with the fruit trees and that large pantry off the kitchen to store your jars?"

Whenever you ask your customers for their opinion, whether the expected response may be long or short, wait for it. Give them time to answer and do not speak again until after they do.

Silence, in fact, is golden. You can't talk and listen at the same time. "Listen" means just that. Listen and concentrate. Do not merely have your mouth closed while your brain is busy formulating your next sentence. You will go through these closing scenarios many times in your sales career and will reach a point where you believe you can anticipate everything a buyer will say. Before you get too complacent, remind yourself that each new buyer is a personality in his own right and may still surprise you. Allow buyers to finish what they have to say; never interrupt or jump in the second one pauses for breath. Apart from being impolite, you might stifle an important statement that could be crucial to your success in closing.

Ask For The Commitment

By means of indirect questions, encourage the buyers to make a definite commitment.

"Would you like to move into this home about the end of next month, or do you prefer to try to move sooner?"

"It seems we've found the perfect home sooner than you expected and I realize you cannot move until school is out. Shall we go ahead and ask for a 90-day escrow which would bring us to the end of May?"

"Remember the house I showed you on Oak Drive? Between that one and this, which of the two do you feel you would enjoy living in the most?"

"Yes, that is a nice refrigerator and I know you wanted a home that included one. If we could get the sellers to change their decision to take it with them, would you want to own this lovely home?"

"You seem concerned about the $10,000 that you might be able to borrow from your parents. We can either make your offer contingent on their agreement, or we could ask the seller if he would be willing to carry that amount and you then make monthly payments to him. Which would you prefer?"

Thinking It Over

"We'd like some time to think it over," says Mrs. Buyer meaning she wants to get out of this house quick before they find themselves signing a purchase agreement on a home that they definitely should buy!

Tell her soothingly that you understand they do not wish to make a commitment until they've thought it through and most people feel the same. Say that you want to be sure they have all the information they need to make their decision and would like them to sit down again while you go over it. This time, seat them in the livingroom or family room (whichever one has the most appeal to them and where they can be comfortable) and patiently reiterate the home's positive features and its benefits to them; the convenience of the location to shops and schools; the attractive neighborhood; how well the payments will fit in with their budget; and, in general, paint a word picture of them living in the home.

Conclude by saying: "I'm concerned about this home being seen by other buyers this weekend who might like it as well as you do and write up an offer. It would be such a shame if you were to lose a home that fits your requirements so well. I know you want to give this more thought so I'm going to leave you here alone and go out to my car. I have some paperwork with me so you can take as long as you like to talk about it. You won't be delaying me at all but I will be right outside if you have more questions." Then quickly get up and go outside.

The buyers are left alone in the house allowing them to experience a pseudo pride of ownership in what could easily be their new home. You have given them the opportunity to "think it over" and make the commitment in privacy. After a suitable interval, return and suggest that you start the paperwork so that the home can be taken off the market as soon as possible.

17

Writing The

Offer To Purchase

*T*he showings are over, the decision is made; the buyers are ready to make an offer to purchase. This is not your cue to let out a sigh of relief, relax into a comfortable chair and fill in contract blanks as fast as you can before they change their minds! No, indeed, how competently you handle the writing of this very important document can very well make or break the deal.

Each State has its own rules and regulations for agents to follow when writing offers to purchase. Laws of a few of them require that this legal document be drawn by an attorney; some States permit only certain preprinted forms approved by the State to be used by real estate licensees; in others the real estate broker can prepare the document and choose the pre-printed form although the majority elect to use those which have been scrutinized by attorneys. When you are responsible for putting a buyer's offer on paper, use a typewriter or handwrite it legibly with a pen, not pencil.

It is vital that you thoroughly understand the provisions of the form your broker uses for the writing of an offer to purchase real estate. Know where to find the clause pertaining to each topic it covers and be ready to answer questions from the buyer. You should, of course, recommend to the buyer that he consult an attorney for legal advice, or a trained accounting professional if he has questions regarding the tax consequences of the proposed purchase.

Licensees are required to give copies of documents and

agreements to those who sign them at the time of execution. Consider, in preparing to write the offer, who will need copies:

1. Listing broker;

2. Selling broker;

3. Buyers: one now and another with the seller's acceptance. If more than one person (other than spouses residing together) will sign the form, each should receive his/her own copies;

4. Copy for seller to keep.

Once the seller has accepted the offer and this acceptance has been communicated to the buyer, the document becomes a contract and you will want to make photocopies of it for the mortgage, title and escrow companies. You will also need copies of the contract for your own file and those of cooperating brokers.

Each blank space above the buyer's signature on the offer-to-purchase form must be filled out either with the appropriate data or with "n/a" to indicate that the item is not applicable to this particular transaction. Printed sentences or paragraphs which do not apply can be deleted by neatly drawing lines through them; such deletions should be dated and initialled by the buyer and seller. Some agents, when completing the form for a nervous buyer, may try to put him at ease by addressing the easier questions first. If you do that, proof reading must be even more careful than usual to ensure no item has been overlooked before the offer is signed by the buyer. The recommended and most straightforward method of completing the form is to go through it and consider each item in the order in which it is printed.

Although the printed wording differs somewhat from one form to another, in general all cover certain components which, together, comprise a good contract. An excellent example is California Association of REALTORS' "Real Estate Purchase Contract and Receipt for Deposit" (DLF-114) which, with permission of the Association, is reproduced on the next four pages. (These forms can be ordered from C.A.R., 525 So. Virgil Avenue, Los Angeles, CA 90020 or those Californa Board offices with supply stores.)

Many of the provisions included in offer-to-purchase forms are self-explanatory but let's consider the ones which agents are more likely to be uncertain about. Starting with city and date: although your office may be located in Smithville and the

REAL ESTATE PURCHASE CONTRACT AND RECEIPT FOR DEPOSIT
(LONG FORM — WITH FINANCING CLAUSES)
THIS IS MORE THAN A RECEIPT FOR MONEY. IT IS INTENDED TO BE A LEGALLY BINDING CONTRACT. READ IT CAREFULLY
CALIFORNIA ASSOCIATION OF REALTORS® (CAR) STANDARD FORM

_____, California, _____, 19____

Received from _____

herein called Buyer, the sum of _____ Dollars $ _____

evidenced by ☐ cash, ☐ cashier's check, ☐ personal check or ☐ _____, payable to _____

_____, to be held uncashed until acceptance of this offer as deposit on account of purchase price of

_____ Dollars $ _____

for the purchase of property, situated in _____, County of _____ California.

described as follows: _____

1. **FINANCING:** The obtaining of Buyer's financing is a contingency of this agreement.

  A. Deposit upon acceptance, to be deposited into _____ $ _____

  B. INCREASED DEPOSIT within_____ days of Seller's acceptance to be deposited into _____ $ _____

  C. BALANCE OF DOWN PAYMENT to be deposited into _____ on or before _____ $ _____

  D. Buyer to   apply, qualify for and obtain a NEW FIRST LOAN in the amount of.......................... $ _____
    payable monthly at approximately $_____ including interest at origination not to
    exceed_____%, ☐ fixed rate, ☐ other _____ all due_____ years from date of
    origination. Loan fee not to exceed _____ Seller agrees to pay a maximum of_____
    FHA/VA discount points. Additional terms_____

  E. Buyer ☐ to assume, ☐ to take title subject to an EXISTING FIRST LOAN with an approximate balance of ... $ _____
    in favor of_____ payable monthly at $_____ including interest
    at_____% ☐ fixed rate, ☐ other _____
    Fees not to exceed_____ . Disposition of impound account _____
    Additional Terms _____ .

  F. Buyer to execute a NOTE SECURED BY a ☐ first, ☐ second, ☐ third DEED OF TRUST in the amount of $ _____
    IN FAVOR OF SELLER payable monthly at $ _____ ☐ or more, including interest at_____% all due
    _____ years from date of origination, ☐ or upon sale or transfer of subject property. A late charge of_____
    shall be due on any installment not paid within_____ days of the due date. ☐ Deed of Trust to contain a
    request for notice of default or sale for the benefit of Seller. Buyer ☐ will, ☐ will not execute a request for notice of
    delinquency. Additional terms_____
    _____

  G. Buyer☐ to assume, ☐ to take title subject to an EXISTING SECOND LOAN with an approximate balance of . $ _____
    in favor of_____ payable monthly at $_____ including interest
    at_____% ☐ fixed rate, ☐ other _____ . Buyer fees not to exceed _____ .
    Additional terms _____ .

  H. Buyer to apply, qualify for and obtain a NEW SECOND LOAN in the amount of .... $ _____
    payable monthly at approximately $_____ including interest at origination not to exceed
    _____% ☐ fixed rate, ☐ other, _____
    _____ all due_____ years from date of origination. Buyer's loan fee not to exceed_____ .
    Additional Terms _____

  I. In the event Buyer assumes or takes title subject to an existing loan, Seller shall provide Buyer with copies of
    applicable notes and Deeds of Trust. A loan may contain a number of features which affect the loan, such as
    interest rate changes, monthly payment changes, balloon payments, etc. Buyer shall be allowed_____ calendar
    days after receipt of such copies to notify seller in writing of disapproval. FAILURE TO SO NOTIFY SELLER
    SHALL CONCLUSIVELY BE CONSIDERED APPROVAL. Buyer's approval shall not be unreasonably withheld.
    Difference in existing loan balances shall be adjusted in ☐ Cash, ☐ Other_____

  J. Buyer agrees to act diligently and in good faith to obtain all applicable financing _____
    _____

  K. ADDITIONAL FINANCING TERMS:_ _____
    _____

  L. TOTAL PURCHASE PRICE .... _____ $ _____

2. **OCCUPANCY:** Buyer ☐ does, ☐ does not intend to occupy subject property as Buyer's primary residence.

3. **SUPPLEMENTS:** The ATTACHED supplements are incorporated herein:
    ☐ Interim Occupancy Agreement (CAR FORM IOA-11)   ☐ _____
    ☐ Residential Lease Agreement after Sale (CAR FORM RLAS-11)   ☐ _____
    ☐ VA and FHA Amendments (CAR FORM VA/FHA-11)   ☐ _____

    Buyer and Seller acknowledge receipt of copy of this page, which constitutes Page 1 of _____ Pages.
    Buyer's Initials (_____) (_____)   Seller's Initials (_____) (_____)

THIS STANDARDIZED DOCUMENT FOR USE IN SIMPLE TRANSACTIONS HAS BEEN APPROVED BY THE CALIFORNIA ASSOCIATION OF REALTORS® IN FORM ONLY. NO
REPRESENTATION IS MADE AS TO THE APPROVAL OF THE FORM OF ANY SUPPLEMENTS NOT CURRENTLY PUBLISHED BY THE CALIFORNIA ASSOCIATION OF
REALTORS® OR THE LEGAL VALIDITY OR ADEQUACY OF ANY PROVISION IN ANY SPECIFIC TRANSACTION. IT SHOULD NOT BE USED IN COMPLEX TRANSACTIONS
OR WITH EXTENSIVE RIDERS OR ADDITIONS.

A REAL ESTATE BROKER IS THE PERSON QUALIFIED TO ADVISE ON REAL ESTATE TRANSACTIONS. IF YOU DESIRE LEGAL OR TAX ADVICE, CONSULT AN
APPROPRIATE PROFESSIONAL.

To order, contact — California Association of Realtors®
525 S. Virgil Avenue, Los Angeles, California 90020
Copyright© 1986. California Association of Realtors®
Revised 12-86

OFFICE USE ONLY
Reviewed by Broker or Designee _____
Date _____

SF-L8-SF

REAL ESTATE PURCHASE CONTRACT AND RECEIPT FOR DEPOSIT (DLF-14 PAGE 1 OF 4)

Subject Property Address _____

4. ESCROW: Buyer and Seller shall deliver signed instructions to _____ the escrow holder, within _____ calendar days from Seller's acceptane which shall provide for closing within _____ calendar days from Seller's acceptance. Escrow fees to be paid as follows: _____

5. TITLE: Title is to be free of liens, encumbrances, easements, restrictions, rights and conditions of record or known to Seller, other than the following: (a) Current property taxes, (b) covenants, conditions, restrictions, and public utility easements of record, if any, provided the same do not adversely affect the continued use of the property for the purposes for which it is presently being used, unless reasonably disapproved by Buyer in writing within _____ calendar days of receipt of a current preliminary report furnished at _____ expense, and (c) _____
Seller shall furnish Buyer at _____ expense a standard California Land Title Association policy issued by _____ Company, showing title vested in Buyer subject only to the above. If Seller is unwilling or unable to eliminate any title matter disapproved by Buyer as above, Buyer may terminate this agreement. If Seller fails to deliver title as above, Buyer may terminate this agreement; in either case, the deposit shall be returned to Buyer.

6. PRORATIONS: Property taxes, premiums on insurance acceptable to Buyer, rents, interest, homeowner's dues, and _____ shall be pro-rated as of (a) the date of recordation of deed; or (b) _____. Any bond or assessment which is a lien shall be ☐ paid, ☐ assumed by _____. County transfer tax, if any, shall be paid by _____. The _____ transfer tax or transfer fee shall be paid by _____. **(Real property taxes will be affected upon transfer of title.)**

7. POSSESSION: Possession and occupancy shall be delivered to Buyer, ☐ on close of escrow, or ☐ not later than _____ days after close of escrow, or ☐ _____

8. VESTING: Unless otherwise designated in the escrow instructions of Buyer, title shall vest as follows: _____

(The manner of taking title may have significant legal and tax consequences. Therefore, give this matter serious consideration.)

9. MULTIPLE LISTING SERVICE: If Broker is a participant of a Board multiple listing service ("MLS"), the Broker is authorized to report the sale, its price, terms, and financing for the information, publication, dissemination, and use of the authorized Board members.

10. LIQUIDATED DAMAGES: If Buyer fails to complete said purchase as herein provided by reason of any default of Buyer, Seller shall be released from obligation to sell the property to Buyer and may proceed against Buyer upon any claim or remedy which he may have in law or equity; provided, however, that by placing their initials here Buyer: (   ) Seller: (   ) agree that Seller shall retain the deposit as liquidated damages. If the described property is a dwelling with no more than four units, one of which the Buyer intends to occupy as his residence, Seller shall retain as liquidated damages the deposit actually paid, or an amount therefrom, not more than 3% of the purchase price and promptly return any excess to Buyer. Buyer and Seller agree to execute a similar liquidated damages provision, such as California Association of Realtors® Receipt for Increased Deposit, (RID-11), for any increased deposits. (Funds deposited in trust accounts or in escrow are not released automatically in the event of a dispute. Release of funds require written agreement of the parties or adjudication.)

11. ARBITRATION: If the only controversy or claim between the parties arises out of or relates to the disposition of the Buyer's deposit, such controversy or claim shall at the election of the parties be decided by arbitration. Such arbitration shall be determined in accordance with the Rules of the American Arbitration Association, and judgment upon the award rendered by the Arbitrator(s) may be entered in any court having jurisdiction thereof. The provisions of Code of Civil Procedure Section 1283.05 shall be applicable to such arbitration.

12. ATTORNEY'S FEES: In any action or proceeding arising out of this agreement, the prevailing party shall be entitled to reasonable attorney's fees and costs.

13. KEYS: Seller shall, when possession is available to Buyer, provide keys to all property locks, and alarms if any.

14. PERSONAL PROPERTY: The following items of personal property, free of liens and without warranty of condition, are included: _____
_____

15. FIXTURES: All permanently installed fixtures and fittings that are attached to the property or for which special openings have been made are included in the purchase price, including electrical, light, plumbing and heating fixtures, built-in appliances, screens, awnings, shutters, all window coverings, attached floor coverings, T.V. antennas, air cooler or conditioner, garage door openers and controls, attached fireplace equipment, mailbox, trees and shrubs, and _____ except _____

16. SMOKE DETECTOR: Approved smoke detector(s) shall be installed as required by law, at the expense of ☐ Buyer, ☐ Seller.

17. TRANSFER DISCLOSURE: Unless exempt, Transferor (Seller), shall comply with Civil Code Sections 1102 et seq., by providing Transferee (Buyer) with a Real Estate Transfer Disclosure Statement: a) ☐ Buyer has received and read a Real Estate Transfer Disclosure Statement; or b) ☐ Seller shall provide Buyer with a Real Estate Transfer Disclosure Statement within _____ calendar days of Seller's acceptance. Buyer shall have three (3) days after delivery or five (5) days after delivery by deposit in the mail to terminate this agreement by delivery of a written notice of termination to Seller or Seller's Agent.

18. TAX WITHHOLDING: Under the Foreign Investment in Real Property Tax Act (FIRPTA), IRC 1445, *every* Buyer of U.S. real property *must*, unless an exemption applies, deduct and withhold from Seller's proceeds ten percent (10%) of the gross sales price. The primary exemptions are: No withholding is required if (a) Seller provides Buyer with an affidavit under penalty of perjury, that Seller is not a "foreign person," or (b) Seller provides Buyer with a "qualifying statement" issued by the Internal Revenue Service, or (c) if Buyer purchases real property for use as a residence and the purchase price is $3000,000.00 or less and if Buyer or a member of Buyer's family has definite plans to reside at the property for at least 50% of the number of days it is in use during each of the first two twelve-months periods after transfer. Seller and Buyer agree to execute and deliver as directed, any instrument, affidavit and statement, or to perform any act reasonably necessary to carry out the provisions of FIRPTA and regulations promulgated thereunder.

19. ENTIRE CONTRACT: Time is of the essence. All prior agreements between the parties are incorporated in this agreement which constitutes the entire contract. Its terms are intended by the parties as a final expression of their agreement with respect to such terms as are included herein and may not be contradicted by evidence of any prior agreement or contemporaneous oral agreement. The parties further intend that this agreement constitutes the complete and exclusive statement of its terms and that no extrinsic evidence whatsoever may be introduced in any judicial or arbitration proceeding, if any, involving this agreement.

Buyer and Seller acknowledge receipt of copy of this page, which constitutes Page 2 of _____ Pages.

Buyer's Initials (_____) (_____)   Seller's Initials (_____) (_____)

┌─── OFFICE USE ONLY ───
Reviewed by Broker or Designee _____
Date _____

SF-L6-SF

REAL ESTATE PURCHASE CONTRACT AND RECEIPT FOR DEPOSIT (DLF-14 PAGE 2 OF 4)

Subject Property Address _____

20. **CAPTIONS:** The captions in this agreement are for convenience of reference only and are not intended as part of this agreement.

21. **ADDITIONAL TERMS AND CONDITIONS:**
ONLY THE FOLLOWING PARAGRAPHS A THROUGH J WHEN INITIALED BY BOTH BUYER AND SELLER ARE INCORPORATED IN THIS AGREEMENT.

Buyer's Initials   Seller's Initials

_____/_____   _____/_____   **A. PHYSICAL INSPECTION:** Within _____ calendar days after Seller's acceptance Buyer shall have the right, at Buyer's expense, to select a licensed contractor(s) or other qualified professional(s), to inspect and investigate the subject property, including but not limited to structural, plumbing, heating, electrical, built-in appliances, roof, soils, foundation mechanical systems, pool, pool heater, pool filter, and air conditioner, if any. Buyer shall keep the subject property free and clear of any liens, indemnify and hold Seller harmless from all liability, claims, demands, damages or costs, and repair all damages to the property arising from the inspections. All claimed defects concerning the condition of the property that adversely affect the continued use of the property for the purposes for which it is presently being used shall be in writing, supported by written reports, if any, and delivered to Seller within_____ calendar days after Seller's acceptance. Buyer shall furnish Seller copies, at no cost, of all reports concerning the property obtained by Buyer. If such reports disclose conditions or information unsatisfactory to the Buyer, which the Seller is unwilling or unable to correct, Buyer may cancel this agreement. Seller shall make the premises available for all inspections. BUYER'S FAILURE TO NOTIFY SELLER SHALL CONCLUSIVELY BE CONSIDERED APPROVAL.

Buyer's Initials   Seller's Initials

_____/_____   _____/_____   **B. GEOLOGICAL INSPECTION:** Within _____ calendar days after Seller's acceptance. Buyer shall have the right at Buyer's expense, to select a qualified professional to make tests, surveys, or other studies of the subject property. Buyer shall keep the subject property free and clear of any liens, indemnify and hold Seller harmless from all liability, claims, demands, damages or costs, and repair all damages to the property arising from the tests, surveys, or studies. All claimed defects concerning the condition of the property that adversely affect the continued use of the property for the purposes for which it is presently being used shall be in writing, supported by written reports, if any, and delivered to Seller within _____ calendar days after Seller's acceptance. Buyer shall furnish Seller copies, at no cost, of all reports concerning the property obtained by Buyer. When such reports disclose conditions or information unsatisfactory to the Buyer, which the Seller is unwilling or unable to correct, Buyer may cancel this agreement. Seller shall make the premises available for all inspections. BUYER'S FAILURE TO NOTIFY SELLER SHALL CONCLUSIVELY BE CONSIDERED APPROVAL.

Buyer's Initials   Seller's Initials

_____/_____   _____/_____   **C. CONDITION OF PROPERTY:** Seller warrants, through the date possession is made available to Buyer: (1) property and improvements thereon, including landscaping, grounds and pool/spa, if any, shall be maintained in the same condition as upon the date of Seller's acceptance; (2) the roof is free of all known leaks and that water, sewer, plumbing, heating, air conditioning, if any, and electrical systems and all built-in appliances are operative, (3) _____ .

Buyer's Initials   Seller's Initials

_____/_____   _____/_____   **D. SELLER REPRESENTATION:** Seller warrants that Seller has no knowledge of any notice of violations of City, County, State, Federal, Building, Zoning, Fire, Health Codes or ordinances, or other governmental regulation filed or issued against the property. This warranty shall be effective until the date of close of escrow.

Buyer's Initials   Seller's Initials

_____/_____   _____/_____   **E. PEST CONTROL:** Within _____ calendar days from the date of Seller's acceptance Seller shall furnish Buyer, at the expense of ☐ Buyer, ☐ Seller, a current written report of an inspection by_____ , a licensed Structural Pest Control Operator, of the main building and all structures of the property, except _____ .

If no infestation or infection by wood destroying pests or organisms is found, the report shall include a written "Certification" as provided in Business and Professions Code 8519(a) that on the date of inspection "no evidence of active infestation or infection was found."

All work recommended in said report to repair damage caused by infestation or infection by wood-destroying pests or organisms found, including leaking shower stalls and replacing of tiles removed for repairs, and all work to correct conditions that causes such infestation or infection shall be done at the expense of Seller.

Funds for work to be performed shall be held in escrow and disbursed upon receipt of written Certification as provided in Business and Professions Code 8519(b) that the property "is now free of evidence of active infestation or infection."

Buyer agrees that any work to correct conditions usually deemed likely to lead to infestation or infection by wood-destroying pests or organisms, but where no evidence of existing infestation or infection is found with respect to such conditions is NOT the responsibility of Seller, and that such work shall be done only if requested by Buyer and then at the expense of Buyer.

If inspection of inaccessible areas is recommended by the report, Buyer has the option of accepting and approving the report or requesting further inspection be made at the Buyer's expense. If further inspection is made and infestation, infection, or damage is found, repair of such damage and all work to correct conditions that caused such infestation or infection and the cost of entry and closing of the inaccessible areas shall be at the expense of Seller. If no infestation, infection, or damage is found, the cost of entry and closing of the inaccessible areas shall be at the expense of Buyer. Other _____

Buyer's Initials   Seller's Initials

_____/_____   _____/_____   **F. FLOOD HAZARD AREA DISCLOSURE:** The subject property is situated in a "Special Flood Hazard area" as set forth on a Federal Emergency Management Agency (FEMA) "Flood Insurance Rate Map (FIRM) or "Flood Hazard Boundary Map" (FHBM). The law provides that, as a condition of obtaining financing on most structures located in a "Special Flood Hazard Area," lenders require flood insurance where the property or its attachments are security for a loan.

The extent of coverage and the cost may vary. For further information consult the lender or insurance carrier. No representation or recommendation is made by the Seller and the Brokers in this transaction as to the legal effect or economic consequences of the National Flood Insurance Program and related legislation.

Buyer and Seller acknowledge receipt of copy of this page, which constitutes Page 3 of_____ Pages.

Buyer's Initials (_____) (_____)   Seller's Initials (_____) (_____)

```
┌─────────── OFFICE USE ONLY ───────────┐
│ Reviewed by Broker or Designee _____ │
│ Date _____                           │
└────────────────────────────────────────┘
```

REAL ESTATE PURCHASE CONTRACT AND RECEIPT FOR DEPOSIT (DLF-14 PAGE 3 OF 4)

Subject Property Address _____
Buyer's Initials   Seller's Initials

____/____   ____/____   **G. SPECIAL STUDIES ZONE DISCLOSURE:** The subject property is situated in a Special Studies Zone as designated under Sections 2621-2625, inclusive, of the California Public Resources Code; and, as such, the construction or development on this property of any structure for human occupancy may be subject to the findings of a geologic report prepared by a geologist registered in the State of California, unless such a report is waived by the City or County under the terms of that act

Buyer is allowed _____ calendar days from the date of Seller's acceptance to make further inquiries at appropriate governmental agencies concerning the use of the subject property under the terms of the Special Studies Zone Act and local building, zoning, fire, health and safety codes. When such inquiries disclose conditions or information unsatisfactory to the Buyer, which the Seller is unwilling or unable to correct, Buyer may cancel this agreement. BUYER'S FAILURE TO NOTIFY SELLER SHALL CONCLUSIVELY BE CONSIDERED APPROVAL.
Buyer's Initials   Seller's Initials

____/____   ____/____   **H. ENERGY CONSERVATION RETROFIT:** If local ordinance requires that the property be brought in compliance with minimum energy Conservation Standards as a condition of sale or transfer, ☐ Buyer, ☐ Seller shall comply with and pay for these requirements. Where permitted by law, Seller may, if obligated hereunder, satisfy the obligation by authorizing escrow to credit Buyer with sufficient funds to cover the cost of such retrofit.
Buyer's Initials   Seller's Initials

____/____   ____/____   **I. HOME PROTECTION PLAN:** Buyer and Seller have been informed that Home Protection Plans are available. Such plans may provide additional protection and benefit to a Seller or Buyer. California Association of Realtors® and the Broker(s) in this transaction do not endorse or approve any particular company or program:
a) ☐ A Buyer's coverage Home Protection Plan to be issued by _____
Company, at a cost not to exceed $ _____ , to be paid by ☐ Seller, ☐ Buyer: or
b) ☐ Buyer and Seller elect not to purchase a Home Protection Plan.
Buyer's Initials   Seller's Initials

____/____   ____/____   **J. CONDOMINIUM/P.U.D.:** The subject of this transaction is a condominium planned unit development (P.U.D.) designed as unit _____ and _____ parking space(s) and an undivided _____ interest in all community areas, and _____ . The current monthly assessment charge by the homeowner's association or other governing body(s) is $ _____ . As soon as practicable, Seller shall provide Buyer with copies of covenants, conditions and restrictions, articles of incorporation, by-laws, current rules and regulations, most current financial statements, and any other documents as required by law. Seller shall disclose in writing any known pending special assessment, claims, or litigation to Buyer. Buyer shall be allowed _____ calendar days from receipt to review these documents. If such documents disclose conditions or information unsatisfactory to Buyer, Buyer may cancel this agreement. BUYER'S FAILURE TO NOTIFY SELLER SHALL CONCLUSIVELY BE CONSIDERED APPROVAL.

22. OTHER TERMS AND CONDITIONS: _____
_____
_____
_____
_____

23. OFFER: This constitutes an offer to purchase the described property. Unless acceptance is signed by Seller and the signed copy delivered in person or by mail to Buyer, or to _____ who is authorized to receive it, in person or by mail at the address below, within _____ calendar days of the date hereof, this offer shall be deemed revoked and the deposit shall be returned. Buyer acknowledges receipt of a copy hereof.

24. AMENDMENTS: This agreement may not be amended, modified, altered or changed in any respect whatsoever except by a further agreement in writing executed by Buyer and Seller.

REAL ESTATE BROKER _____   BUYER _____

By _____   BUYER _____
Address _____   Address _____
Telephone _____   Telephone _____

ACCEPTANCE

The undersigned Seller accepts and agrees to sell the property on the above terms and conditions.
Seller has employed _____
as Broker(s) and agrees to pay compensation for services as follows: _____
Payable: (a) On recordation of the deed or other evidence of title, or (b) if completion of sale is prevented by default of Seller, upon Seller's default, or (c) if completion of sale is prevented by default of Buyer, only if and when Seller collects damages from Buyer, by suit or otherwise, and then in an amount not less than one-half of the damages recovered, but not to exceed the above fee, after first deducting title and escrow expenses and the expenses of collection, if any. Seller shall execute and deliver an escrow instruction irrevocably assigning the compensation for services in an amount equal to the compensation agreed to above. In any action between Broker and Seller arising out of this agreement, the prevailing party shall be entitled to reasonable attorney's fees and costs. The undersigned acknowledges receipt of a copy and authorizes Broker(s) to deliver a signed copy to Buyer.

Dated _____ Telephone _____   SELLER _____

Address _____   SELLER _____

Real Estate Broker(s) agree to the foregoing.

Broker _____ By _____ Date _____

Broker _____ By _____ Date _____

OFFICE USE ONLY
Reviewed by Broker or Designee _____
Date _____

REAL ESTATE PURCHASE CONTRACT AND RECEIPT FOR DEPOSIT (DLF-14 PAGE 4 OF 4)

buyer's present residence is in the suburb of Jonesboro, you may actually be writing the offer with the buyer while still at the house he has chosen in Pottstown where he will sign it; it is Pottstown which will appear on this line. Similarly, if you were to prepare the offer in your office in accordance with written or telephoned instructions received from an out-of-town buyer and then mail it to him for signature, you would insert the name of the town in which it will be executed. When filling in the date, write the month in full; numerals can be misleading since the first number indicates month in some cases and day of month in others.

Earnest Money

When you write a name on a contract the first time, always ask for the spelling. It is appropriate, and more professional, to use legal names on this legal document rather than the abbreviated versions (or nicknames) which people tend to use in less formal aspects of their lives. You may feel you know how to spell "John Brown", but you could learn later that your buyer's legal name is "Jonathan T. Braun", or you thought you were working with Mary Thompson but discover she's really Marie Ann Tomson.

An offer-to-purchase form usually doubles as a receipt for the buyer's earnest money. At some time in the future, it may be necessary to be able to identify the person(s) entitled to refund of earnest money if the contract fails. Some forms provide a space in which to write the name of the person who provides the earnest money and a separate line on which to state the names of the person(s) who will be included on the title. When using this type, in the blank following "Received from" write ONLY the name of the person(s) signing the check, not the names of all the buyers.

Other versions of the offer-to-purchase form have one space which does the double duty of receipting for the earnest money as well as to indicate the names of those who will hold title. In this case, if more than one buyer is involved, it is suggested that you insert the name of the person(s) actually signing the check or promissory note followed by: "on behalf of" and add the other name(s). For example,

> "Received from Jonathan T. Braun on behalf of himself and Marie Ann Tomson"

In some areas, it is commonplace to insert a description following the names, i.e. "husband and wife", "brothers", "unmarried persons", etc.

A common question you will be asked by buyers is the amount required for earnest money. Generally they want this to be as little as possible. You, as the sellers' representative, know that it is prudent to obtain a respectable amount to indicate that the buyers are serious in their desire to own the property; in some instances, the earnest money is the liquidated damages the sellers retain in the event of default by the buyers. If you suggest an amount, you may then be asked if that much is necessary; it is better to offer a choice:

"Sellers like to have an earnest money deposit of ten per cent of the purchase price. We're talking about a home in the $130,000s so a deposit of $13,500 would be about right, or would it be more convenient for you to invest $12,500 today?"

If the buyer balks at the amount you request, explain that you feel his offer will have a better chance of acceptance when accompanied by a substantial earnest money deposit. Sometimes you will be told that there are insufficient funds in the buyer's account for a check of that amount to clear. Suggestions you might make include:

(a) Buyer can write the check for the amount he wishes to tender but advise him to expect a request from the seller for an additional sum in a counteroffer;

(b) Buyer should write a check for an amount that will clear and ask his permission to indicate on the document that the earnest money will be increased within a certain time period after sellers' acceptance of the offer (specify amount to be added and number of business days);

(c) Use of a promissory note;

(d) Buyer can write check for amount that will clear and make up the difference with a promissory note.

During qualifying you prepared the buyer for the moment when he would be making an offer to purchase and explained the advisability of having a checkbook with him when looking at homes. Even so, buyers do not always remember this. Keep a supply of promissory note forms in your briefcase and a note can be used for the earnest deposit instead of a check. Indicate on it that the note will be redeemed as soon as buyer is notified of seller's acceptance, or on the next business day. Give the buyer a carbon copy of the note with "Copy" written across its face. A signature is required only on the note itself and you should specifically tell him NOT to sign the copy.

You will sometimes have buyers who get very nervous when asked for a substantial earnest money deposit. This should not, of course, be allowed to develop into an argument; you try for the maximum amount but gracefully accept the figure with which the buyer is comfortable and is willing to tender. As long as the consideration has some value (even as little as one dollar!), it is technically acceptable because there is no requirement of adequacy to make a contract enforceable. However, few real estate professionals feel comfortable when presenting an offer accompanied by a marginal amount of earnest money and it would be of small consolation in an action for specific performance. Do your best to tactfully persuade buyers to tender a reasonable amount of earnest money and note on the form the manner in which it is paid, i.e. cash, personal check, promissory note, etc.

Do not be surprised one day if your buyers want to use personal property as consideration; this could take the form of diamonds, art, boat, car, etc. Provided that the item has value, it is legally acceptable and should be described in detail on the offer. It is the sellers' prerogative to decide whether such consideration is acceptable to them or not but you should certainly recommend that this type of deposit by appraised by a qualified concern.

Description Of Property

Custom in your area should be followed when filling in the property description. The important factor is that the description clearly identifies the property to be purchased without leaving any doubt in anyone's mind. Sometimes the street address is sufficient, other areas use both street address and legal description; in rural areas, you may find that a metes and bounds identification is required. Should you find yourself faced with a lengthy legal description, to avoid error in copying it by hand or typewriter, it is a good idea to make photocopies of it from the deed or other reliable document and attach them to the offer.

How Title Is To Be Taken

The manner in which title is to be vested is not a simple decision and is one upon which buyers often need to seek legal and/or tax counsel. Certainly you, as a real estate agent, cannot and must not advise what is best in their particular circumstances. You can explain in general what the options are (i.e. community property, joint tenancy, tenancy in common, tenancy in partnership, etc.) but **never** make any attempt to interpret their effect upon your buyers.

If they have not pre-determined how they wish to take title, this is no reason to delay writing the contract. Simply add a clause into "Additional provisions" stating that buyers agree to notify title (or escrow) company within a specified time period how they wish to go into title on the property.

There will be times when you may be working with a buyer who intends to have someone else on the title but cannot, or does not desire to, name the second party at time of writing the contract. In that event, add "and/or assigns" after name of buyer. To avoid delay in escrow, add a clause under the section for "Additonal Provisions, Terms & Conditions" such as:

"Should buyer elect to add or substitute names of other persons in the manner title is to be taken, buyer agrees that such names shall be furnished in writing to title company no later than (number) business days prior to closing date."

Price

The tricky $64,000 question! By now the buyers are very much aware of the listed price and have probably given you their opinion about it. If they have made no objection to this figure, or if you have been able to convince them that the house is priced at fair market value, you might say, "Shall we write this up at $(list price)?"

In "hot" real estate markets in which a new listing is quickly gone, some agents will even write the listed price into the appropriate blank and proceed to discuss the buyers' plans for financing the purchase. It is my opinion that this is rather presumptuous but, if you ever do that and find you were too confident and must alter the figure to reflect the buyers' intended offer, draw a neat line through the numbers written, insert the revised price and ask the buyers to initial and date the change before proceeding further. This should be done any time you have to alter something on the form.

When you believe that the buyers do not intend to offer full price, review comparable sales with them again before you ask for the amount they want to offer. You might then say, "Mr. and Mrs. Buyer, you've given me the impression that this is truly the home you both feel is right for you and your family. We've gone over the prices recently paid for homes in this neighborhood. I imagine that you want this offer to be accepted so that you will soon be able to start living in this lovely home. What price would you like to offer the sellers now?"

The reply you receive could be, "What's the least you think they'll take?"

Even if the sellers have indicated a figure to you that they might accept, they have not officially lowered the price so this is not information that you (as their agent or subagent) are at liberty to reveal. You can only encourage the buyers to make their best offer and could respond:

"It is always possible that the sellers will accept a serious offer. They are aware of recent sales, just as you are, so have a good idea of what their home is worth. I personally feel that it is fairly priced and can only recommend that you make your offer at, or close to, the listed price."

Bargain Hunters

At times you will come across dedicated bargain-hunters who want to make an offer on a listed property at a price you cannot, in all good conscience, justify or recommend that the sellers accept. As a real estate licensee, you are obligated to present all written offers from interested customers to the seller even if the price specified is so low you are embarrassed to do so. The only exception to this policy is when sellers have given the listing broker written instructions not to take them any offer below a certain price (or other parameter). So, if Mr. Bargain Hunter insists you write the offer for him, you must do so. Pause and put your pen down. It's time to exercise your powers of persuasion.

If yours is an active market, point out the possibility that another agent could be writing an offer on this same property today. Tell Mr. Bargain Hunter that his offer and the other one will probably be presented to the seller at the same time and, assuming all other terms and conditions of the two contracts are equal, ask him which of the two he would accept if he was the seller. Then ask if he wants to take the risk of losing this home.

Another argument concerns the value of Mr. Bargain Hunter's own time. Point out that he has spent (number) hours with you to find this home which he has told you he really likes and which seems to most closely meet his expressed needs. At the income level he has previously indicated to you, that time represents an investment of $........ (time multiplied by approximate hourly rate of income). Ask him if he really wants to take the chance of losing that investment by having you take to the seller an offer which, in your educated opinion, stands no chance of acceptance.

Your answer from this Mr. Bargain Hunter may be that the seller can always make a counteroffer. Agree that this is true but explain that as the offer is so far off the fair market value of the home, the seller may not wish to enter into negotiations with him. The seller may feel insulted that the buyer does not consider his home of greater worth or may feel he is not dealing with a serious purchaser. Then say, "Wouldn't you prefer to increase the chance of owning this lovely home by making a higher offer now?"

First Time Buyers

First-time buyers are faced with a commitment to purchase the most expensive item of their lives. Seeing in writing what appears to them to be an astronomical number can cause panic. They feel compelled to make a much smaller offer and you must overcome their fears with reassurance.

During your discussions, you will have learned how Mr. and Mrs. First Time plan to finance the home and will have figured out estimated monthly payments for them. Write down on a sheet of paper now what monthly payments will be at the listed price, at the figure they are now suggesting and at steps between the two. Show them your figures and point out how a small extra amount paid each month can make a big difference in the price they can afford for the home. Help them realize how much better their chances are of owning this home if they will agree to pay a little more each month. It is much easier for insecure buyers to relate to monthly payments than it is for them to adjust their thinking to the total price of the home.

Financing

Be very specific about how the buyer intends to fund the purchase. It is extremely helpful to the agent writing the offer if the form being used for the purpose has just about every possible method set forth in the pre-print; the California Association of REALTORS form is ideal in this respect.

There are forms in use, however, on which the preprint states: "The purchase price shall be $......... payable as follows" and you are confronted with a large blank space in which to describe the financing details. The most efficient way to fill the space is by enumerating each item. This system clearly indicates the amounts to be provided from each source and you can easily add them up to make sure the total coincides with the purchase price offered. As an example, let's consider how this blank might be filled in on a form in which the buyers want to assume the existing first mortgage:

> The purchase price shall be $.......... payable as follows:
>
> 1. $.......... hereby receipted for;
>
> 2. $.......... (approximately) payable by cashier's check upon delivery of deed;
>
> 3. $.......... (approximately) by assumption of existing first mortgage on the property. Purchaser agrees to assume and pay said loan currently payable in monthly installments of $.......... including principal and interest at the rate of ....% per annum. Purchaser agrees to make application to (name of lender) to assume said loan no later than five business days after Seller accepts this contract, execute all documents and furnish all information and documents required by the lender and pay the customary costs of such assumption.

The word "approximately" appears after the amounts because, when you write the document, you do not know what the exact balance of the loan will be on the day it is assumed. This will be figured during escrow proceedings.

If the preprint on the form you are using does not so specify, it would be necessary to add at the end of Item 3 wording to cover the terms on which the buyer agrees to assume, i.e. pay a loan transfer fee not to exceed a certain dollar amount and, if the lender has the right to increase the interest rate upon assumption, state the maximum rate the buyer will accept. Similarly, if not covered in your form's preprint, in the best interests of both buyer and seller, add a sentence which gives both parties the option to void the contract if buyer's loan assumption (or new loan) has not been approved by a specific date.)

Whenever any action is required by the buyer, protect seller's interests by specifying when it is to be completed. The buyer should understand that if any action set forth in the contract to be performed by him is not done by the date shown, the seller has the right to cancel the contract. In the example, buyer is required to apply for loan assumption no later than five days after the contract has been accepted; name of lender to whom application must be made is given and you have described the type of days so that it is not left open to interpretation whether these are calendar days or business days. Five **business** days would cover the period Monday through Friday or Thursday through Wednesday, and, if a legal holiday fell on any of those days, the period would be extended. Five **calendar days** means five consecutive days, i.e. Monday through Friday or Thursday through Monday.

Possession

It is natural for a purchaser to want possession of the property on the date of close of escrow. On the other hand, the seller may want to be sure that escrow does indeed close before going to the expense of moving. The subject of date of possession should be agreed upon at the time the offer and acceptance are made in order to avoid future problems for all concerned. If the owner will not vacate the house on or before close of escrow, the purchaser's interests should be protected by covering the hold-over period, even if it is only a few days, with an after-sale occupancy agreement in which is set forth a per diem rate and conditions.

Personal Property

It should be understood by all concerned which items of personal property your buyers expect to receive with the purchase of the home. If you are the listing agent as well as selling agent, you will be aware of the sellers' intentions in this respect and can inform the buyers accordingly. Those who are handling only the selling end of a transaction seldom have the advantage of having read the listing agreement and should be especially alert concerning personal property.

Preprinted forms usually include at least a list of permanently attached items commonly found in the average house. In the case of kitchen appliances which are not built-in, note on the form their brand names and serial numbers or description.

Look around the house to see if there is anything that should be mentioned in the contract for the buyers' (and your own) protection. There may be a very nice diningroom chandelier and people get very attached to these. You have not been told by the listing agent that the sellers plan to take it when they move but, on the other hand, it is not safe to assume that it will be sold with the home. Play it safe and add the chandelier to your list. Finish the paragraph with words similar to, "All of these items of personal property are present in the house as of today's date and shall all be in good working condition on date of delivery of deed."

Sometimes you do know that a particular item of personal property has been excluded from the sale but the buyers fall in love with it anyway. The fact that it is going to be removed becomes a bone of contention and presents you with a seemingly unsurmountable objection. In that case, give the sellers a chance to consider selling the home to these buyers by including the item on the contract with the other personal property. In addition, it is politic to draw the sellers' attention to this excluded item by writing into "Additional Provisions, Terms & Conditions" a paragraph stating that the buyers are asking for it (or, if applicable, that contract is contingent upon the item being included in the sale).

Additional Provisions, Terms Or Conditions

This section of contract forms is a catch-all to cover matters for which there is no printed paragraph. The following is a check-list of items you may periodically find it necessary or convenient to include here:

1.   Advice on manner in which title is to be taken;

2.   Clauses covering anything upon which the contract is contingent, all of which should specify a termination date, such as:

    a) approval by co-purchaser(s), (spouse or others);

    b) approval by an attorney and/or tax consultant;

    c) structural inspection;

    d) satisfactory cost estimate of work buyers want to do at their expense;

    e) sellers to perform certain work or replace specific items;

    f) sellers agreement to include specific item(s) in sale;

    g) sale and transfer of another property owned by the buyers to third party;

    h) buyers being successful in obtaining financing (if not adequately covered elsewhere in the form);

      i) reading and approval by buyers of any by-laws, declarations, rules and regulations or other documents pertaining to subject property.

3. Applicable disclosures, i.e.

    a) fact that buyer (and/or seller) is a real estate licensee;

    b) an ownership interest held in subject property by listing and/or selling agent or broker;

    c) written confirmation of pertinent facts about property previously disclosed verbally to buyers and/or sellers;

    d) confirmation of agency status of the real estate licensees involved in the transaction.

Quite often, preprinted forms allow insufficient space for items you want to include in this (or other) section. Attach a page (with sufficient copies) to the document and reference it in the contract as being a part of same.

Time For Acceptance

How should you select a date by which the sellers must either accept or reject an offer? Time is of the essence all around so you don't want to stretch the waiting period out. Your buyers are entitled to know as quickly as possible whether or not their offer has been accepted. It is to your sellers' advantage, too, to make a decision without undue delay because the buyers can withdraw their offer prior to notice of acceptance.

Before entering a random date (or number of days) in the pertinent blank, try to determine the accessibility of the sellers. If the home is listed with another agent, telephone for this information. When it is your own listing, you should have a good idea already. Always instruct your seller to notify you when he will be out-of-town, even overnight. You want to avoid having the contract fail, for example, because the sellers are away for the weekend and cannot be contacted before time for acceptance expires. The buyers may be disheartened if you have to go back to them with no answer and a request for an extension; if buyers' remorse has set in, they will probably decline.

Should you be unable to determine the sellers' availability, explain to the buyers that you are not sure how quickly you can reach the sellers. Ask for a minimum of three days, longer if the buyers are willing, but if they do not want to allow more than 48 hours, suggest that another provision be added to the effect that should sellers' agent be unable to reach them personally or by telephone to convey the offer during that period, the offer shall automatically be extended a further 24 hours.

Signature

Signatures of buyer(s) and agent who is preparing the offer will complete this document ready for presentation to the seller. You will be signing it on behalf of your employing broker whose name (company) usually appears on the line above. If the selling agent, employed by Home & Hearth Realty, is writing the offer on a property listed by ABC Real Estate, appropriate wording above the agent's signature would be, "Home & Hearth Realty (in cooperation with ABC Real Estate)".

The form will also have spaces for completion by the seller and the listing broker. Some selling agents misunderstand what is needed in those and try to complete them when preparing the offer. Obviously, a selling agent associated with one company cannot have any certain knowledge of the amount of commission the listing broker's office has negotiated with the seller. When you are on one side of a transaction as the selling agent, all you actually know about the commission is the percentage of sales price that the listing broker is offering to another broker who successfully procures a buyer. Leave those blanks alone!

Give your buyers copies of the offer and ask them to read it over. While this is being done, go through it again yourself to be sure there are no errors and that every blank (except the ones just mentioned) has been completed with pertinent information or "n/a" (not applicable). Try to review it as though you are a third party checking it at a future date; if you can disassociate yourself from it, you will be more apt to spot any items which are open to interpretation. Clarify them in writing now in keeping with the buyers' intentions.

When the buyers have gone all through the document, ask if everything meets with their approval. Remind them that if they are in need of tax or legal advice concerning the proposed purchase they should consult the appropriate professionals before executing it. If the buyers are satisfied with the document you have prepared, ask them to sign it and initial each page.

You will probably have a situation occasionally when one of the persons who want to buy the house is present during the writing of the offer but it is not possible for the spouse or other partner(s) in the purchase to attend. In order for the offer to be valid, the signature will be needed of any person who is named in the offer as being a buyer but sometimes the other parties are out-of-town. To avoid delay in presenting the offer to the seller, you can cover this situation in "Additional Provisions" with wording similar to:

"This offer is contingent upon approval of same in writing by other named buyer(s), specifically (name or names). This approval shall be in the form of signature(s) on copy(ies) of this document which shall be transmitted by express service to the office of sellers' agent (agent's company and address) and, if not received by midnight of (date), this contract shall be null and void and all monies hereby receipted for shall be returned to purchaser."

Pave The Way For A Counteroffer

If you feel that the offer is unlikely to be accepted by the sellers, prepare the buyers for a counteroffer. You could say,

"I'll get this to the sellers right away so that we can see how they react to your offer. If they feel they cannot accept it just the way it is now, they may decide to write a counteroffer. Let's see what happens."

When the buyers want terms which deviate from the sellers' indicated wishes and the offer is below list price, ask which is more important to them, the sellers' acceptance of price offered or another concession they are requesting. For example, the buyers may also want the sellers to carry a second mortgage and/or leave personal property which has been excluded from the sale. You could mention that, in your opinion, it is unlikely that the sellers will be willing to make both a price concession and the other one, too.

The buyers' response to your comment (or to a direct question) may reveal which is most important to them, acceptance of the lower price offered or agreement with the other request. This will help you negotiate the offer with the sellers when they, as you had anticipated, will not go along with the offer as it stands but may be persuaded to agree to one concession or the other.

A few buyers may even have second thoughts and delete

their demand for the personal property after you make your comment. Then, when you meet with the sellers, if they are upset about the lower price, you can point out that the buyers had also intended to include this other request but agreed to omit it in hopes that the sellers would accept the amount offered. You could mention that a counteroffer which includes a higher price, could possibly result in the buyers countering with their request for the personal property item to be included.

Conclude The Meeting

Once the document has been executed, bring the meeting to an end by telling the buyers you want to get their offer to the sellers as soon as possible. The longer you remain in the their company, the greater your chances are of having to change the offer or have to resell the buyers on having made the right decision.

If your buyers have a good sense of humor, you might jokingly warn them they may soon find themselves experiencing symptoms of an ailment known as buyer's remorse. Assure them there is no need for alarm because this is quite common among buyers who are on tenterhooks waiting to hear if their offer has been accepted. You might even give them a piece of paper on which you have earlier typed a "prescription" or a pill bottle containing M&M's or candy mints labelled "Buyer's Remorse Pills".

Contract Writing Seminars

The ability to prepare a well-written contract, one in which the intents of all the parties are completely understood by everyone who will be involved in the real estate transaction, is a skill which should be mastered by every licensee. No matter how many years you have been in the profession, or how proficient you believe you are, it is always a good idea to periodically attend a seminar on contract writing especially the ones sponsored by your State Association.

18

Negotiating Between The Principals

The buyers have agreed to buy but, before you can say you have a deal, the sellers must agree to sell. A contract that will have a good chance for a successful conclusion should contain benefits for both parties and the real estate professional must become a skilled negotiator.

Custom in each market determines who will present the offer to the sellers unless the latter have specified otherwise in the listing agreement. In your market, the system to be followed by the selling agent may be one of the following:

1. Contact the listing agent and arrange to turn buyers' offer over to listor who will present it to the sellers;

2. Contact the listing agent and make an appointment to go together to present the offer to the sellers;

3. Contact the sellers direct and present the offer yourself. This would apply if the offer is on one of the selling agent's listings and, in some markets, even if it is not.

If you cannot reach the appropriate person, you should contact the listing broker for direction and assistance in getting the offer to the sellers as quickly as possible.

In this chapter, we are assuming that you are the listing agent and will be the one to present the offer to in-town sellers. As we have said a number of times in this book, preparation is all-important and will certainly influence your success with the seller. Your first task, then, is to read over the document with an eagle eye; if it is one prepared by another agent it needs a complete digesting and analysis by you to determine how closely it fits the sellers' objectives. Don't take anything for granted; even if it was written by someone who has been in the business a number of years, you cannot count on contract writing being one of that agent's strong points. In fact, a new agent who has recently taken a contracts course might bring you a better-written document. When the offer is one which you prepared yourself, it is advisable to double-check to see that you overlooked nothing; further, you now need to read the document from the viewpoint of the sellers instead of the buyers.

Here is a check list:

1. Is the handwriting legible?

2. Is the date correct? When an offer is written in early January, see if it reflects the correct year.

3. What is the price offered? Can you justify it? Where does it fall in the price range indicated by your own CMA?

4. Consider the earnest money and manner in which it is submitted. If it is by promissory note, what is the redemption date? How will that affect the sellers? Is the amount adequate?

5. Does the buyers' proposed financing fulfil the terms of the listing agreement? Do the totals of the various financing amounts plus earnest money equal the purchase price being offered? If the buyers are to apply for financing, are date(s) given by which loan application must be made and approval obtained?

6. Are the proposed dates for close of escrow and possession going to fit in with the sellers' objectives?

7. Is the manner in which title is to be vested indicated?

8. Are the buyers requesting that any personal property be included in the sale other than what is customary?

9. Are there any contingencies? If so, are dates indicated on or before which waiver must be made by buyers? Will any contingency require clarification? Be sure you have all the information needed to give sellers an explanation.

10. How much time do the sellers have to consider this offer?

11. Are there any areas of the offer which are open to interpretation which should be clarified in writing?

12. Do you need to make extra copies of the document so that each of the sellers will have one to read as you are going through it?

13. Have the listing and selling agents made proper disclosure of their agency status to the principals?

As you read over an offer to purchase, imagine yourself reading the same document one week prior to closing. Consider if there are any clauses that you would wish had been spelled out more clearly at the time it was written; if your answer is affirmative, now is the time to get this document cleaned up. An agent can never make any changes to a document without the authorization of the principals so, during your study of the offer, merely observe what needs to be brought to the sellers' attention and consider appropriate wording for amendments you anticipate they will want to make. There will be times when you will receive from another agent a document which has more than its share of errors and/or omissions; bring it to the attention of your broker who may wish to contact the broker at the selling agent's office and request that the document be redone and signed by the buyers again.

Finally, consider the overall offer. Is it a good one? Do you feel it would be in the sellers' best interests to accept it, or, at the very least, make a counteroffer to the buyers? If your answer is affirmative, you should do your best to point out the advantages to the sellers and help them overcome any objections they may have. On the other hand, if you truly feel that it is not the best one that can reasonably be expected in the time frame in which the sellers have to get the property sold, you should express your opinion and substantiate it with facts. Keep in mind that the sellers' time frame does not necessarily end on the same date as your current listing and the offer should be judged impartially on its own merits, not as one which possibly represents your last chance to make a sale before the listing expires!

Preparing For Price Objection

Many times, the price offered is below listed price. You will find a "deck" of cards which you will make up now a good tool to have when the time comes to discuss the offer with the sellers. Prepare the deck on blank 3"x5" cards; it is more effective to use a different color for each card category enumerated below (a mail order source for anyone who cannot find these in local shops is Quill Corporation, 100 S. Schelter Road, Lincolnshire, IL 60069).

1. Figure out approximately what the sellers' net proceeds would be with a full price sale and write that number with a felt marker pen on the first card. On a back corner, index the card for yourself in pencil with the notation, "Full price net proceeds", and continue to put similar cues on the back of each card you do. Work out the net at the price offered and show that figure on another card of the same color.

2. Figure the difference and write the amount on card #3.

3. If the sellers are going to be moving on a predetermined date, regardless of what happens with present house, estimate the monthly costs of mortgage interest, property taxes, insurance, yard care, utilities and other necessities that will be a continuing expense for the sellers as long as they own it. Itemize these on card #4 and show their total. Multiply that total by two, three and four months and put those three amounts on card #5.

4. If the listing agreement indicates that the sellers are willing to sell the house to buyers using a new VA loan and the offer is based on conventional financing, estimate the cost to the sellers of VA financing and put it on a card. Consider any other savings the sellers will realize by accepting the present offer (for example, the amount saved by not having to buy a new chandelier); make cards for each one, the more the better.

5. Look up recent sold prices on comparable homes in the neighborhood and put each one on a separate card Indicate on these, where applicable, if government or seller-carry financing was involved. Show the period of time each one was on the market.

6. When the property is your own (or office) listing, you should have a record of the number of showings it has had and prospects' reactions. Put on a card the number of days this house has been on the market and the number of showings, i.e. 31 - 9. On the reverse side of this card, write or type overall reactions.

7. Select numbers at random between price offered and listed price (perhaps at even thousands) and figure the

amount each price would add to the sellers' net proceeds and display on cards.

Set Up Appointment With Sellers

Time is of the essence so make an appointment with Mr. and Mrs. Seller for the same day, if possible, next day at the latest. Sellers very often want to know right away "how much" and this, or other details of the offer, is information you do not want to reveal over the telephone. An exception, of course, would be when sellers are away and will not return before buyers must have their answer.

When the offer is below listed price, as it often is, and the sellers know the amount prior to your meeting, they may develop negative feelings towards the buyers before even reading the full details. If it's a full price offer, there may be some contingencies that you suspect the sellers will resist; advising the price over the phone and then going into the contingencies when you arrive may cause a let-down and perhaps some resentment.

The easiest way to avoid the problem is to ask your office secretary or an associate to make the appointment for you, but, if you have to make the call yourself, be ready to tactfully postpone answering sellers' questions. You might say:

"I'm calling from a restaurant with people all around so I think it's best not to go into that right now. I'd like to bring the offer right over. Is that convenient or would you prefer me to come later this afternoon?"

"This pay phone is at a gas station and I'm having trouble hearing you. As you suggested, I'll be at your house at 7 o'clock and we'll go over the papers together.

"Mr. Seller, I'm calling you from a pay phone and someone is waiting here to use it. I'd like to come right over and you can see the entire offer. I can be at your house in 15 minutes. Okay?"

"Mrs. Seller, I have to get details from the selling agent. I'll have complete information for you when I come by at 7."

If the contract was written by another agent who will not be with you when you present the offer, check to see if that agent will be available by telephone during your appointment with the sellers.

Establish Rapport With Sellers

Mr. and Mrs. Seller are likely to be awaiting your arrival in a state of anticipation and anxiety. They want to get the property sold or they would not have put it on the market; however, unless they are living in a house they truly dislike, they may be feeling somewhat apprehensive. Is this move, which will become a reality once they accept an offer, really the right decision to make? Be prepared to handle a case of "sellers' remorse"! Their reasons for selling may be voluntary or due to a job transfer but, if they have lived in their house for any length of time, it holds many memories for them. They may be ready to move on to the next stage of their lives but letting go of an old friend is never easy. If the offer you are going to present is off the listed terms in any way (lower price, certain contingencies, etc.), Mr. and Mrs. Seller may feel this indicates criticism of their home and will feel compelled to rise to its defense.

When you arrive at the sellers' home, make every effort to institute and maintain a relaxed atmosphere for your presentation. Suggest that you sit down together around the kitchen or dining room table, not in the livingroom which is too formal. An around-the-table gathering creates an aura of a family discussion and is more convenient for looking at paperwork together. Devote a minute or two to small talk to establish rapport and then get down to business.

First, tell Mr. and Mrs. Seller a little bit about Mr. and Mrs. Buyer, mention some of the features they especially liked and the reason this is the home they want to own. If a person has a beloved pet he cannot take with him to his next home, he feels much better about parting with it when he knows he has found it a good home with people who will also love it; it's a similar situation with a house.

Next, pass copies of the offer to each concerned party and, before you go into any details, allude to the price. From the moment typical sellers learn you have an offer for them, their goal is to know the price figure; there is nothing to be gained by keeping them in suspense. You might prefer to direct their attention to the overall benefits of the offer but they would not be concentrating on what you are saying because they would be scanning the document to find that magic number.

Selling The Sellers

Full price offers with no contingencies are the ultimate dream of real estate agents but do not come along too often.

In this instance, we will assume that you are presenting one which you believe is good overall but will require some selling on your part. You have anticipated sellers' objections and have arrived prepared to overcome them.

Price Is Too Low

If you are presenting an offer below listed price, tell the sellers that you realize they may be disappointed with the figure but, before discussing it, you would like to go all through the entire document with them so that they have an overall picture. As you go along, stress the positive points:

"These people want a very quick closing which makes it possible for you to go ahead with your plans for the new house you've already chosen and be settled in well before Christmas".

"You'll notice that the buyers have a very substantial down payment and are well-qualified to purchase this home. We don't have to worry about them being able to get bank financing and they are not asking you to carry a second mortgage for them."

"Mr. and Mrs. Buyer loved your diningroom chandelier and understood completely why you intend to take it with you."

By the time you've gone through the offer, you may have convinced the sellers that the buyers are not really thieves and do have some good characteristics!

When you reach the end of the document, the sellers may be willing to concede that the offer does have some good points but they still have difficulty with the reduced price. They are probably doing mental arithmetic, subtracting price offered from listed price and telling themselves there is no way they will come down that much.

Make certain you have their full attention and ask Mr. and Mrs. Seller if their main objection to this offer is the price. When you are told it is, explain that the difference between listed price and price offered is not as much as it may seem at first glance because what really counts is the amount of money they will have in hand after the close of escrow. Tell them that you are going to show them an estimate of the true dollar significance represented by this offer and one for full-price.

Produce your deck of cards and deal out those which illustrate the difference in net proceeds. Point out that the lower figure is what they can expect if they accept this offer, but the higher figure may or may not ever be forthcoming. Ask if they are prepared to risk their future plans by waiting for a full-price buyer.

Turn up the card which shows what the waiting period could cost them in holding costs, delayed move and maybe even loss of earnest money already invested in another home (if purchase was not contingent on prior sale of this one); mention the inconvenience to them of more showings here. Point out the problems that can arise when owners have to move before a house is sold.

Lay down your cards with miscellaneous savings this offer represents and show them how much it adds to their net proceeds. Mention that even if another buyer is found who will pay more, he might make demands they would not appreciate such as owner financing, a lengthy escrow period, and/or stipulate that the chandelier remain.

Go on to the comparable cards and remind them what recent sales have been and, if applicable, how some of those numbers should be adjusted to reflect financing and other considerations that those sellers had to contend with which are not called for in this offer.

The Counteroffer

The sellers may still be unwilling to accept the offer as it stands and it is time to suggest that, by means of a counteroffer, there is no need to totally reject it either.

Ask the sellers to name the figure at which they are willing to transfer ownership to these buyers. It is very possible that you will be asked to assist in this decision but do avoid being the one to name that number! When they tell you the figure they will accept, write it on a counteroffer form; complete the page by adding any other amendments or clarifications to the offer requested by the sellers. The new figure will obviously have narrowed the gap between listed price and price offered. Why not give the sellers one more chance to accept the buyers' offer as it stands? Turn again to your cards, select the one that is closest to the sellers' new price, and say:

"Mr. and Mrs. Seller, before I ask for your signatures, I want to be sure that you understand you are about to put the ball back in the buyers' court. Right now they are waiting to hear whether you have confirmed their decision to buy this home for themselves by accepting their offer as it stands. If you do that, you then have a firm contract and can proceed with your new plans.

"If, instead, you send them this counteroffer, they will have the right to decide whether or not I can phone you tomorrow and tell you your house is sold. Today, **they** are the ones in suspense. Once you sign this form and I take it out the front door, **you** will be the people on pins and needles! The buyers can choose to accept the increased price, counteroffer or merely walk away and buy someone else's home. Let's go over once more what's at stake here."

Lay down the card which shows the addition to net proceeds the new price would bring. Draw their attention again to the card depicting monthly holding costs and figure out for them how much time the increase in proceeds represents. Mention that even if they wait, the next buyers may not be willing to pay even the counteroffer figure and they will have gambled and lost.

Take the offer and the counteroffer and lay the signature pages side-by-side in front of the sellers. Tell them the decision is theirs. Give each one a pen. Then remain silent until they have executed and dated one or the other, not both. When the sellers elect to go with the counteroffer, do not permit them to sign the offer as well.

Financing Objections

When your sellers object to the buyers' proposed arrangements for financing, it is usually because a cost to sellers is involved as is the case with some forms of government financing. Know the amount of this cost in advance so that you can explain to the sellers how much money is involved and what that amount represents in holding costs, etc., if they refuse the offer for this reason.

The offer may require sellers to carry a second mortgage although, on the listing agreement, they specified cash only terms. The sellers may have listed the property in that manner because the full proceeds of the sale are needed for another home purchase. They are unlikely to accept this offer as written so try to keep the transaction alive with a counteroffer which indicates that the offer is acceptable if the buyers will obtain financing from another source. In the case of sellers who really need the sale and want to motivate these purchasers to proceed with the transaction under the new terms, you could suggest that they consider making a concession on the selling price. Your counteroffer might read:

"1. Sellers will not carry a second mortgage.

2. In the event that purchasers elect to obtain financing from other sources, price will be lowered to $_____.

3. Purchasers agree to act diligently to obtain said financing. In the event that loan approval is not made on or before (date) and sellers so notified in writing by purchasers, either party may terminate this agreement unless extended in writing."

If the sellers do not actually have an immediate need for the entire proceeds of the sale, suggest to them that, before rejecting this offer, they should discuss with their tax advisor its effect on their income tax obligation. There is always the possibility it could be to their benefit to accept the offer but only a qualified tax person can properly advise them on the consequences.

Ask the sellers, too, what their main objection is to carrying financing for the buyers. You might be able to suggest a counteroffer amending the terms to suit the sellers so that they would agree to carry a second.

Contingency Objections

During preparation for this presentation you went over the "Additonal Provisions" section of the contract carefully. If a termination date for any contingency has not been provided, draw this to the sellers' attention. There is no point in taking the house off the market if no time limit is specified for Aunt Mary to approve her nephew's purchase and, a few days before closing, she comes to town, looks at the house and tells him to forget this one and find something else!

If you find anything at all that is left hanging, tell the sellers that you feel it would be advisable to add an addendum before signing the offer. A wide-open sentence such as, "This contract is contingent upon inspection of the subject property by Mrs. Mary Porson", should be clarified to read:

"This contract is contingent upon inspection of the subject property by Mrs. Mary Porson. The inspection shall be made no later than ten calendar days from date of sellers' acceptance of this offer. Purchasers shall notify sellers in writing no later than 5 P.M. of the tenth day if they do not wish to proceed with this purchase. If such notice is not received, this contingency shall be deemed waived."

Another contingency that you will have to tackle at times is the buyers' wish to have an item included in the purchase that the sellers are not willing to leave; diningroom chandelier, mirrors, riding lawnmower, refrigerator, etc. are items that often become bones of contention. A method by which you can help the sellers relinquish their desire to take the item with them is to find out what it would cost to replace the item, write it down on a card and use similar arguments as you did with the price objection.

Sometimes an item has sentimental value to the sellers and there is no way they will part with it. Ask them if they would be willing to make a price allowance so that the purchasers can get one of their own choice. If they agree, draw a line through that provision and replace it with, "Sellers agree to make an allowance of $300 for purchasers to replace existing diningroom chandelier which is not included in sale."

You will be confronted fairly regularly with an offer which is contingent upon the sale of buyers' present home. Few sellers are willing to take their property off the market and wait for this event to occur. If the buyers' other terms are acceptable, suggest a compromise to your sellers which might be worded:

"This contract is contingent upon sale and successful close of escrow of purchasers' present residence at (address). However, sellers retain the right to leave (address of sellers' house) on the market for sale during the term of this contract unless buyers notify them in writing that this contingency is removed. If sellers receive another offer to purchase that is acceptable to sellers, buyers shall be notified in writing and have 48 hours from receipt of notice to remove the contingency by furnishing written waiver to sellers. If the contingency is not removed within that time, this contract shall be considered null and void and earnest money will be refunded to purchasers."

An amendment can either be written on the offer or contained in a counteroffer. However, if there are a number of items that the sellers wish to address, it is far better to prepare a counteroffer because a cluttered contract is more likely to result in future errors or misunderstandings. Even the smallest addition, deletion or amendment must be initialled and dated by each seller and buyer.

We would like to have all our presentation appointments conclude with sellers' acceptance of the buyers' offer but, if you leave with a counteroffer or rejection, keep smiling and assure the sellers that you will continue to do your best to get their property sold.

Presenting The Counteroffer

Although Mr. Seller, who reluctantly countered with a price below list, sent you on your way with the words, "Tell those people that's the lowest I'll take!" ringing in your ears, as the diplomat you are, you do not approach the buyers with that attitude! If you paid heed to Mr. Seller's heated instructions and told them, when they refused to accept sellers' counteroffer, that the latter absolutely will not lower the price any further, you could easily cost the sellers a sale. There is always the chance you will be able to persuade the buyers to raise their offer and will be taking a counteroffer from them to the sellers. Meanwhile, you hope the sellers will have thought over your remarks about price which they may have been too upset to acknowledge when you presented the offer. Perhaps they will have cooled down by your next meeting and be quite receptive to the new counter. It's your job to protect the sellers from the consequences of their own emotions.

At the time buyers ask an agent to write an offer which does not fully comply with listed terms (few do) the agent should prepare those buyers for the possibility of a counteroffer. If you did this, your call to say you have one to present will not come as a shock. You might say:

> "Mr. Buyer, the sellers have carefully considered your offer to purchase their home. They could not accept it as written but are interested in working this out. They have written a counteroffer and I want to go over this with you. May I bring it over now, or would seven o'clock be more convenient for you?"

Again, you should try to evade any telephone discussion of the terms of the counteroffer.

By agreeing to accept the buyers' below-list price or compromising on a contingency, as the case may be, the sellers have made a concession. Reaching the stage at which both buyers and sellers are satisfied is a matter of give and take. Do your best to overcome the buyers' reluctance (if any) to accept the concession by repeating persuasions already discussed in Chapter 16. If the counteroffer is not acceptable to the buyers, suggest that they offer another written compromise to the sellers.

You now have a counteroffer for the sellers which should be closer to their original wishes. Encourage them to accept this revised offer by patiently going over once more:

(a) positive aspects of the entire offer;

(b) owners' motivation for selling;

(c) current market situation; and

(d) possibility that further procrastination will cause buyers, who must have a definite contract on a house within a limited time frame, to withdraw from negotiations and look for another property.

Hopefully, you will leave the sellers this time with an accepted contract to deliver to buyers and can proceed to get the transaction closed.

Initials Required

When you have presented an offer to the sellers, or a counteroffer to them or the buyers, whatever the recipients elect to do with it (accept, reject, amend or counter), the tendering principals must be promptly notified of the other parties' decision.

For example, perhaps the original offer was accepted by the sellers but it was necessary to clarify the document in handwriting in certain places. Go back to the buyers and announce right away that the sellers have accepted and signed the offer. Tell them that you just need to go over with them a few items which were not entirely clear and get their approval. Point out the changes and, if the buyers are agreeable, ask them to initial and date each one. This must be done by each person named on the document as one of the principals.

19

From Contract
To Closing

$\mathcal{M}$any potential pitfalls lie on the path between acceptance of contract and transfer of title. It is imperative that you monitor this stage of your transaction very closely every step of the way.

The manner in which buyers' earnest money deposit must be handled is set forth in the laws of each State. Usually, the broker is required to place the deposit in a trust fund account at a bank or other recognized depository. Sometimes the earnest money is held by a neutral entity who is appointed to handle the escrow proceedings and, occasionally, the deposit goes directly to the sellers. Your broker will advise you how the earnest money you received from the buyers is to be handled in keeping with State law and office policy.

The title commitment and escrow work should be ordered promptly. In some States (Colorado is an example) it is the custom for a title company to provide both title insurance (at sellers' expense) and document preparation, the latter under the direction of the listing broker at his expense. In this case, the closing department of the title company is, in fact, acting as a "secretary" for the broker and most contact with the principals will be made through the broker. In other areas such as California, where the cost of escrow is the responsibility of the buyers and/or sellers as specified on the contract, the party(ies) paying choose which company to use; however, a real estate agent is often asked to make a recommendation. An agent of the escrow company will contact both buyers and sellers to prepare written escrow instructions in keeping with the agreed-upon terms of the contract. The real estate agent should be in touch with the person who is doing the escrow or preparing the documents at least once weekly to stay on top of progress of the work and be ready to lend a hand to round up various tardy documents, remind principals of acts or paperwork required from them, etc.

Go through the contract and make a list of items and dates by which each of its provisions are to be met. Note the contingencies and obtain written, signed waivers as soon as appropriate to distribute to all concerned parties (i.e. principals, brokers, escrow agent, mortgagee). Get in the habit of checking this form DAILY to determine if there is any action required of you that day to help move the transaction smoothly along to its conclusion.

Your local multiple listing service should be notified by use of the appropriate form as soon as you have an accepted contract (if you are the listing agent). It may, at first, be a contingent contract which, subsequently, will change to pending and then sold after close of escrow. Send each change to MLS as it occurs; you depend upon the accuracy of multilist statistics when preparing market analyses so do your part in keeping those statistics current.

If it is the custom in your area to hold a formal closing at which both buyers and sellers are present, find out in advance which hours of the day are best for each person (including the cooperating real estate agent). Try to set the date and place of closing to suit the majority. If any of the buyers and/or sellers will not be available to sign the appropriate documentation and will be represented by an attorney-in-fact, a copy of the power of attorney should be furnished to the escrow company at least a week prior to closing.

Working Towards Closing With The Buyers

Once you have sellers' signatures on an accepted offer-to-purchase, the first order of business is to deliver a copy to the purchasers. Remember, until purchasers are notified of such acceptance, they have the right to withdraw the offer so telephone them immediately and deliver the copy promptly, the same day if possible. Put a note in your file showing the time you telephoned notice of acceptance and ask purchasers to sign a receipt when you give them the copy of accepted contract.

Prepare a list for the purchasers showing everything they are required to do to comply with the terms of the contract and the date by which each item must be completed. Keep a copy in your own file and telephone the buyers to give them advance reminders of upcoming contract deadlines outlined on the list. Follow up to be sure that deadlines were met and mark them off on your checklist.

Ask the buyers to which lender they intend to apply for financing and remind them to obtain an insurance policy for their new home. The lender will require evidence of insurance before funding the loan and not many buyers assume the sellers' policy. When a condominium is being purchased, a certificate pertaining to the master insurance policy for the building will be needed so find out from the condominium manager which company issued it and contact that company for the certificate.

If the subject property is covered by any by-laws, declarations, and/or rules and regulations, obtain a set and deliver it to the buyers to read and approve as called for in the contract. Get a signed and dated receipt for your file. Follow the same procedure in connection with any other data the contract calls for the buyers to receive.

The buyers should arrange, in ample time, for transfer of funds to complete the downpayment. Many buyers do not realize how long it can take to release funds from stockbrokers, credit unions and other sources; out-of-area buyers who intend to tender a personal check must deposit it with the escrow holder a sufficient number of days in advance to allow the funds to clear. Check with the escrow officer for the time period needed and advise the buyers accordingly; it is good practice to reconfirm in writing so as to have a copy in the file.

Make arrangements for the buyers to walk through the home again shortly before title is to transfer. Get buyers' signatures on a statement indicating that this walk-through was done and everything was satisfactory; if there are any problems, get them resolved as quickly as possible so that closing of escrow will not be delayed.

Remind the buyers to contact the appropriate utility companies to arrange for service in their names and to discontinue it at their present address, if necessary.

Working Towards Closing With The Sellers

Contact the sellers after you have delivered the accepted contract and advise them that escrow proceedings are about to begin. Follow up with a phone call at least once weekly to let them know what has been accomplished and what you hope to see done in the coming week. It is not necessary to provide an account of any problems that arose and were overcome but the sellers should be made aware of anything that may delay or adversely affect the closing of the contract.

There will not be a great deal for the sellers to do, but you should be prepared to provide assistance and reminders to them as necessary. Depending upon the requirements of your local government, you may have to arrange for inspections and reports to be done covering structural pest control, sewer, well, zoning compliance, etc., and coordinate timing with the sellers.

If the contract calls for sellers to provide a home owner's warranty, advise them of the policies available and costs involved; help them to order the one they prefer. Remind the sellers to notify the utility companies of the date they will be vacating the house so that final bills can be tendered.

As mentioned before, you will find it is much easier to work with informed sellers. Some agents tend to overlook the sellers once the accepted contract stage is passed. Yet the sellers are the people most vitally interested in what is happening ... and, in most instances, it is the sellers who will be paying your commission.

Working Towards Closing With The Lender

Call the lender to whom the buyers are making application for a mortgage and speak with the loan officer who is handling it. Introduce yourself and ask to be contacted whenever the officer needs any assistance or information which you may be able to provide, or if any problems arise. Telephone that person regularly to inquire if anything is needed and check on the progress of loan processing. Have the buyers furnished all documents the lender requires? Are verifications of employment, deposit, etc., coming back on time? It may be necessary for you to contact buyers' employers with a request that the verifications be completed and returned; this is the type of item that can get buried in a busy personnel clerk's in-basket.

Find out from the loan officer the name of the person who will be appraising the property. Telephone the appraiser and make an appointment to meet at the subject property when the appraisal is done. It could be vital to your sale that the appraisal comes in right, i.e. not below a certain figure, so prepare a typed sheet of comparable sales, the more recent the better; real estate agents have better access to the latest sales that may not have been published yet and would not be uncovered by the appraiser's research. If there was a sale of a similar home in the neighborhood at a low price, indicate the reason, i.e. condition, less desirable lot, financing, sale to relative, etc. Take this information with you to the appointment and give it to the appraiser before you leave. This should be done with great tact because you do not in any way wish to give the appraiser the impression of trying to influence the appraisal or of indicating how the job should be done! You might mention that you realize how busy appraisers are and thought that the data on the sheet might save him/her some time.

Close Of Escrow Gift

When the title has been transferred to everyone's satisfaction, it is appropriate to show your appreciation for having had the opportunity to be of service to the principals. If the property was your listing and you sold it, recognize both sellers and purchasers; if you represented one or the other, direct your attention to that party.

Write a nice thank you card to the sellers and/or buyers and send or personally deliver a suitable gift. Suggestions for such gifts include flowers, house plant, case of wines, cheese or fruit basket, souvenir book about the town, framed photograph of the home, key safe, local dining-out coupon book, etc.

Tell The Neighbors

After escrow has closed, with the permission of the principals, call the neighbors and tell them briefly about the sale and the family who will be moving in.

Of course, you will be asked the sales price which gives you an opportunity to talk about values and suggest that, with no obligation at all, they may be interested in having you do a market analysis on their homes. Ask again for leads on neighbors who may be thinking of selling their homes. The average neighbor either has no idea what others are doing or will not pass along the knowledge to an agent; however, there is generally at least one person who is not only full of information but delighted to share it with you, too.

Whether or not you gain any leads from your conversations, follow up each and every one with a handwritten notecard. Thank the owner for taking time to chat with you and ask him to call you whenever he has a real estate question or when (not if) you can be of assistance to him in connection with real estate. Finally, add these names to your list to receive periodic mailings and other contacts.

20

Condominiums &

Residential Lots

*I*n the foregoing pages, we have concentrated on the marketing of single-family homes but there will be times when you may be working with owners and buyers of other properties. Although these could include mobile homes, business opportunities and commercial real estate, these are specialities and will not be covered in this book. However, as a licensee focusing on residential real estate, it is very probable that you will be listing and selling condominiums and residential building sites. An overview is provided in this chapter.

Condominiums

The condominium lifestyle often represents both the first and final stages of a person's tenure as a homeowner. Condos are chosen by young adults initially because of their affordability or perhaps because a complex has a reputation for its social whirl. A condo is a perfect starter home for newly-weds and, after their futures have blossomed and they have progressed on to one or more houses over the years, the older American may turn again to condo-living for its security factor and the freedom it offers from home-care responsibilities.

Condominium complexes range from highrise buildings downtown in the heart of America's biggest cities to rambling, low-profile buildings in the suburbs. At resorts such as Kauai, Palm Springs, Lake Tahoe, Aspen and Hilton Head, condos are an important source of housing. Complexes can be very basic or can feature lavish grounds and recreation facilities. Prices run a complete gamut from the least one could expect to pay for a roof over one's head to incredibly expensive for luxury units in prime locales.

When you work with buyers or sellers of condos, there are certain facts of which you must be aware which distinguish this phase of real estate marketing from the sale of a single-family home.

Legal Documents

In a sense, condo living is akin to being a resident in a small community, When Mr. and Mrs. Buyer purchase a condominium unit, they have a fee simple interest in, and a deed to, the airspace in their own unit plus an undivided interest in the common areas and facilities of the whole complex.

At the time Mr. and Mrs. Buyer take title, they automatically become members of the homeowners' association (HOA) for the complex whether they would choose to or not. The HOA has a board of directors which is responsible for governing the association's business affairs. The board is elected from candidates, who are also owners in the complex, by vote of the HOA members; each condo unit is usually eligible to cast one vote but, sometimes, if certain units are much larger than the others, those may have more than one vote and will also pay a bigger monthly portion of the annual assessment. The elected board usually hires a management company, or employees, to handle the association's bookkeeping and the day-to-day operation and maintenance of the complex.

Every condominium complex has its own set of legal documents known as "By-Laws And Articles of Declaration" written specifically for it at the time it was developed and, possibly, amended as time passed. These define such matters as ownership rights and obligations, election and duties of the board of directors, assessments, etc. Many complexes also draw up rules and regulations which must be observed by residents whether they are owners or tenants. The latter might include rules about the use of the swimming pool, visitor parking, color of drapes in unit windows, rental policies, pet policy, use of signs, etc.

You can readily see that buyers must read these documents thoroughly and, by the same token, so must you. There is no faster way for a real estate agent to make instant enemies on the HOA board than to display a broker's "for sale" sign on the complex grounds, or in the window of a just-listed unit, when the rules forbid this. Further, can you imagine the dilemma you would be in if you sold a unit to buyers who have three cherished Persian cats in a complex which permits only one pet per unit?

As the listor, you must obtain copies of all the pertinent documents in the early days of the listing period. The sellers may have copies available that they were given when they purchased the unit but, to be sure these are current, it is better to get copies from either the management company or a title company. Read them over carefully and have extra sets available for selling agents to peruse and to give to the purchasers. As a selling agent, it is recommended that you have a working knowledge of the documents covering units in different complexes because you are bound to receive questions from buyers.

Few buyers are willing to take time to wade through these lengthy documents before you show units to them. They have not selected the complex in which they will live and will usually want to wait until they do so. When it is time to make an offer, your customers are unlikely to be aware of the documents' exact contents. Even if you do have copies handy in your briefcase, they are far too long and complex to be read and approved on the spot.

The purchasers of a condominium unit must be given the means and opportunity to read and approve the By-Laws and Articles of Declaration before close of escrow so the offer-to-purchase must contain a contingency. It is suggested that you insert in the section for "Additional Terms & Conditions" a paragraph similar to the following:

> "This transaction is subject to the provisions of the By-Laws and Articles of Declaration of the (name of complex) Homeowners Association. Upon acceptance of the contract, sellers shall provide copy of the foregoing documents, together with copy of the rules and regulations of the Homeowners Association, to the purchasers who shall have five business days to approve same. If they do not approve them, they shall so notify sellers in writing before the end of that period and this contract shall then be null and void and all monies hereby receipted for shall be returned to purchasers."

Although this wording requires that the sellers furnish the documents to the purchasers, it will be their agent's responsibility to follow through and see that this is done. It is suggested that you prepare a simple receipt to be signed and dated by the purchasers when the documents are given to them.

Receipt of copy of the following documents pertaining to the (name of complex) Homeowners Association is hereby acknowledged:

(1) Articles of Declaration;

(2) By-Laws;

(3) Rules and regulations.

Purchasers signature _____

_____

Date _____

If you will be giving the material to the selling agent to take to the buyers, prepare three copies of the receipt and get the other agent's signature when you deliver them and ask that the copy with the purchasers' signatures be returned to you promptly. Keep this in your file as a record of when the five days commences.

Assessments

Owners of condominium units pay monthly dues to the homeowners association for maintenance and repair of the building and grounds, insurance, etc. After an annual budget for the complex has been prepared and approved, the amount of dues each owner will be assessed is determined proportionately according to the total number of units. When a complex includes units of different sizes, this is usually taken into consideration. As listing and/or selling agent, you need to know the monthly assessment (dues) so that it can be included in the offer to purchase. Determine, too, if an advance against dues is required at close of escrow. Your wording could be:

"All owners of condominium units are required to pay monthly dues imposed by the (name of complex) Homeowners Association. The amount of these dues is currently $......... per month. Purchaser shall, at close of escrow, deposit $.........

with the Association to be held as security for future assessments which may be due from time to time and for association working capital."

The annual budget usually includes an amount for reserves to build up a fund for use when a major repair (a new roof, for example) is required. Sometimes it does not, or the fund may be insufficient, and a special assessment from unit owners will be necessary when major work has to be done. The listing agent should contact the management company (not just ask the owner) to find out if there is presently a special assessment or if one is anticipated. A selling agent should telephone the listor prior to writing the offer to obtain this information.

If the answer is affirmative, the situation must be covered in the offer to purchase. It must be agreed in writing between purchaser and seller which one will pay the assessment, or balance of same. Obviously, this is a point for negotiation, but it has been my experience that an assessment for a major repair already done or in progress is paid by the present owner and any balance due is held out at close of escrow. Similarly, if the swimming pool heater is inadequate and needs to be replaced soon, it is generally the present owner's expense. However, if the association has voted to add a tennis court to the complex and owners will be assessed for each unit's share of the cost, this is more likely to be borne by the purchaser who should be informed of such plans before making a final decision to buy in that complex.

When you find yourself working regularly with buyers and sellers of condominiums, it is very useful to make up folders containing complete information for every complex in your area.

Building Sites

An agent who lists and/or sells a residential lot should first visit the local building department and pick up all handouts available concerning building requirements in general. Consult with a department representative to confirm the zoning of the subject lot and ask if there would be any problem in getting a permit to build on it. Inquire if special compliance will be needed and get data about height restrictions, building setbacks, required yardspace area, etc.

Of course, one must know if city water, sewer, gas and electrical services are available for the lot. If not, check on alternatives such as well, septic tank, propane gas, etc., and ask the building department if these are permitted in that location.

When the use of a septic tank will be necessary, it is common for the buyer to write an offer contingent upon satisfactory percolation tests. Find out if the lot has any easements running across it and if it has satisfactory access. Note its topography and consider potential building problems, ways to overcome them and the cost factors.

Sometimes you will take a listing for a lot that is located among several others which have not been developed. It is critical to know **exactly** which lot you have listed and be able to show a potential purchaser its boundaries.

People who are looking for a building site want the same information regarding local schools, churches, shopping, transportation, taxes, etc., as those who buy existing homes. Be prepared to furnish this data. You may be asked what is going to be built adjacent to the lot or across the street; be sure you can substantiate your response or simply say that this is not yet known but the present zoning will allow (type of structure) to go there.

Publicity Opportunity

Whenever you sell a unique home or building site, or if the previous owners were celebrities, send news releases to local media. Never miss a chance to get publicity for your real estate accomplishments; people enjoy associating with winners and it is yet another way to increase your business.

21

On The Road To
Real Estate Success

*B*y the time you reach this chapter, you should have your farming well underway and have experienced the joys of listing and selling residential property. In other words, you are truly up and running in real estate sales. Nevertheless, there will come those times in your career when you feel depressed and still have a few doubts about your future success. This final chapter is especially for reading on such occasions, a reminder of the basic, easy-to-overlook steps which we must always continue to cover whether we are novice, intermediate or advanced in our chosen field.

The role of a real estate agent is not unlike that of an actor or actress. There is a "script" for every scene and the dialog varies only a little from one performance to the next. Qualifying buyers, showing homes, closing the sale, you hear the same objections voiced time and again; the words may differ but the substance is your cue. You learn the answers and the "lines" come naturally to you. Sellers who entrust you with the sale of their homes and buyers who come to you for help in finding the right one are casting you in the leading role of their own "dramas". When you are "on-stage" with them, you should be well-prepared and informed, neatly-dressed, pleasing to be with and, of course, always smiling.

The most important asset a real estate professional can have is a good attitude. For some fortunates, this is something with which they are born but, for most of us, it is something we have to cultivate and nurture.

Attitude Towards Customers and Clients

First impressions can be lasting impressions so get off to a good start. Greet your customers and clients with a welcoming smile and a firm handshake. Establish eye contact at the same time and, whenever you are speaking directly to them, try to maintain this contact. When they are talking to you, look straight at them while you listen and occasionally nod your head to show you are paying attention.

Do listen carefully. What these people say, or even what they avoid saying, can reveal hidden objections or give you clues as to how you can help them reach the decision to act. If you are shutting out their words while you mentally formulate what you want to express as soon as the speaker pauses for breath, you are not being a good listener.

Although you may consider them mistaken, if you act as though the customer or client is always right, you can't go far wrong with them. In other words, never disagree with their opinions. Once you allow yourself to get at odds with the customer or client, you weaken your own position. The script here reads, "I understand how you feel. Others have felt the same way. However, ..."

Perhaps you've heard the comment, "buyers are liars ... and sellers are worse". It is usually voiced by a licensee who has had a difference of opinion with a customer (or client) regarding each one's interpretation of something that happened in the course of a real estate transaction. You will probably never have cause to share that opinion if: (a) you properly qualify buyers; and (b) you discipline yourself to cover everything in writing that you say or do in the course of a real estate transaction. Confirm any information you give to a customer and/or client, either in person or by telephone, in a follow-up letter and put copy of same in your file; keep a record sheet of daily happenings in connection with your transactions on file; be very careful to fully complete listing and offer-to-purchase documents in detail.

Other Real Estate Agents

In all your dealings with fellow agents, apply the Golden Rule. Treat them with the courtesy and consideration that you would like to receive in return. Let them know that you welcome their cooperation when you have a listing; when you show their listings, phone them afterwards and give them some feedback. Always be most careful not to step between an agent and his seller or agent and her client.

Get to know agents at other offices as well as your own by participating in activities organized by your local Board. Arrive early to meetings and circulate before they begin. Join Board committees; you will be welcome, newcomer or not.

Yourself

There are days when we are elated and there are those others when we wonder if we're in the wrong business. Accept these ups-and-downs and don't allow yourself to get discouraged. Jot down in a diary the good, encouraging things that happen to you in the course of your professional life and cheer yourself up by reading it again on the down days. Those good days will be back, believe it.

When nothing seems to be happening in your career, make it happen! Read this book again to remind yourself what you should be doing. Do it!

Some States require licensees to have a number of hours of continuing education before their licenses will be renewed. Even if you do not have to meet such a requirement, make a habit of attending lectures whenever you can. If you get only one idea out of each session to help you advance your career, your time has been well spent; chances are, you'll come away with several and your batteries will have been recharged. Stay for the question and answer period, sometimes this is the most valuable segment of the event. As soon as you are eligible, begin studying for a broker's license; it may not be your immediate intent to open your own office but this credential is a worthy accomplishment of which you can be very proud.

Mark the dates on your calendar of the annual conventions sponsored by your State Association and the National Association of REALTORS. These events attract top speakers and you will have the chance to meet and exchange ideas with agents from many other areas. Study for professional designations offered by the industry such as Graduate REALTORS Institute (GRI), Certified Residential Broker (CRB), etc.

Associate with agents who are winners not whiners. Many people get into real estate because they have the misconception that it is a quick and easy way to become wealthy. When they discover their mistake, they do not leave quietly; instead they sit in the office taking the time of any agent who will listen to their tales of woe. Most winners are ready to give a helping hand to newcomers who are in real estate for the right reasons, who have the right attitude and want to get ahead. They have no time to spare for the whiners. You shouldn't either.

Don't become a workaholic with no time to spare for activities with family and friends. Treat yourself to a well-deserved annual vacation and several two- to three-day mini-vacations; schedule personal time each week in your daytimer. You'll be revitalized and glad you stopped to smell the roses on your road to real estate success!

Earlier in this chapter I compared your role to that of an actor or actress. There is one big difference. When the curtain rises on a new production, the performers hope for a long run; when the real estate curtain rises on a brand-new escrow, we look forward to a very quick close. From one good trouper to another then, break a leg!

A novel marketing idea? (Page 103)

REAL ESTATE FARMING:
Campaign For $uccess

by P. J. Thompson, GRI

The Ultimate Farming Handbook
for every Real Estate Agent!

Review from "REAL ESTATE TODAY", June, 1986
- Official publication of NATIONAL ASSN. OF REALTORS -

"This comprehensive handbook explains how to organize a real estate farm for listings, sales and referral business. **Packed with valuable information for the real estate professional, the pages of ideas and how-to advice are applicable to anyone who is working and keeping in touch with prospects.** From the beginning of the book, which stresses planning and organizing, to the end, which gives a critique of farming strategies, **the author provides the salesperson with the necessary motivation to attain a rewarding career in real estate.**

"Thompson, a former journalist, is vice president of a California brokerage and is a licensee in Colorado and California. She **clearly demonstrates the art of writing good letters** as well as the mechanics of designing and organizing newsletters, classified advertising bulletins and neighborhood directories. **Limited budgets can be stretched** when a salesperson follows the author's do-it-yourself copy preparation and takes advantage of the U.S. Postal Service's more economical services outlined in the book. Her experience in design, composition and layout provides useful and practical tips for the real estate salesperson. The actual examples are suitable for salespeople to adapt in their own businesses.

"The most helpful portion of the book is the part about the breakdown of monthly goals in order to keep in touch with the farm residents. The author explains **how to select the right location and size for a geographic farm, organize its paperwork, plan a campaign, and then follow through with it.** Thompson shows the step-by-step work of a salesperson through a one-year campaign. **Even the most experienced real estate professional will find the book loaded with helpful ideas and suggestions.**

"With tips on telephone techniques and door-to-door calling, Thompson shows that farming is an ongoing project; it requires diligence, thoughtful planning, and, most important, perseverance."

Reviewed for "Real Estate Today" by K. Nolte-Obert.

ORDER FORM - PAGE 202

BOOK ORDER FORMS

Contact Kricket Publications for special prices when ordering 12 or more copies.

Kricket Publications
P.O. Box 91832
Santa Barbara, CA 93190

Name _____

Company _____

Ship to office _____ *(or) home* _____ *:*

Street _____

City _____ State _____ Zip _____

Quantity	Title	Each	Amount
_____	Real Estate Farming: Campaign For $uccess	$12.95	_____
_____	Up And Running In Real Estate Sales	$17.95	_____
		Sub-total:	$

Shipping/handling:
1st book $2; add 25 cents
for each extra book _____

California residents: 6% tax *(on sub-total only)* _____

Payment enclosed (check or m.o.) ..... $

Name _____

Company _____

Ship to office _____ *(or) home* _____ *:*

Street _____

City _____ State _____ Zip _____

Quantity	Title	Each	Amount
_____	Real Estate Farming: Campaign For $uccess	$12.95	_____
_____	Up And Running In Real Estate Sales	$17.95	_____
		Sub-total:	$

Shipping/handling:
1st book $2; add 25 cents
for each extra book _____

California residents: 6% tax *(on sub-total only)* _____

Payment enclosed (check or m.o.) ..... $

Mail order to:

Kricket
Publications

P.O. Box 91832
Santa Barbara, CA 93190
Ph. (805) 962-2557